Grievance: In Fragments

Grievance: In Fragments

Grant Farred

PRICKLY
PARADIGM
PRESS

Prickly Paradigm Press, LLC

5751 S. Woodlawn Ave.

Chicago, IL 60637

www.prickly-paradigm.com

ISBN: 9781734643541

Library of Congress Control Number: 2024944688

Printed in the United States of America on acid-free paper.

Grievance is dedicated to the two finest minds in the Commonwealth of Pennsylvania: (Monsignor) Robert Caserio and Jeff Nealon. Interlocutors par excellence, thinkers given, in equal measure, to seriousness and irreverence. To the seriousness of irreverence.

The work on grief owes a great deal to the late Ron Juffer: January 1, 1937–December 17, 2021. Athlete, teacher, artful dissembler. In Ron Juffer there was to be found the very best of northwestern Iowa.

It is senseless to want to say everything at once.

—Karl Jaspers, *The Psychology of Worldviews*

Contents

Preface

Grievance: In Fragments began life as a recognizable formal essay. That mode of writing obviously did not survive. The object of critique, the recurrence of white grievance across US history, remained constant, but the form that the critique assumed did not.

Designating grievance the unimpugnable sovereign claim made by white America demanded a mode of argument incompatible with formal explication. As their sovereign right, those *Grievance* names the aggrieved insisted on a mode of writing appropriate to their sense of injury and felicitous to their singularity.

Grievance emerged as a writing that could only have been provoked into life by the aggrieved: as a series of pointed addresses, intense in its compactness, punctuated as if to insist that the aggrieved could only be addressed in contracted, always connected bursts. Grievance, then, was thinkable only in the most economic phrasing. As such, this writing dictated not only brevity but also its own variation in contraction. It came, as if in rapid bursts, as shorter, sometimes very short, sometimes slightly longer insights, but never too long. Sometimes as pronouncements, sometimes in the form of sharp, concatenated interrogatives. One line of inquiry leading, sure of itself (too sure, one wonders?), to another and then another.

However, the shorter writings, the aphorisms, are related to the (relatively) longer meditations, the fragments, in particular ways: they echo each other; they find not only resonance but also expansion, adumbration, and, on occasion, even contradiction in each other. Brevity, of course, is not the enemy of repetition. *Grievance* does try to hew to the Deleuzian principle that repetition is only useful when it repeats as difference.

Generally, in their referentiality, the aphorisms and the fragments are more likely to substantiate each other, because, in their thinking grievance, in their profiling the aggrieved, they are not true to Karl Jaspers's maxim that it is "senseless to want to say everything at once." Instead, the aphorisms and the fragments try to say one thing that, it is hoped, finds development as the writing unfolds—always with the possibility of surprise at how or where, or maybe even when, such development takes place.

Consequently, the image that is faint in an aphorism might assume a bolder outline in a later aphorism or fragment. The resemblance between one line of critique and another may emerge in an unexpected form, in an entirely unlikely articulation. The same with contradictions. They may present themselves where least expected or emerge in toned-down echoes, audible only in a frequency so restrained that they have to be drawn out, sometimes unwillingly. That which was foreshadowed in one aphorism takes on a completely discontinuous cast in a later fragment. Or, the fragment brings to mind an aphorism that seems incompatible with it.

Sometimes an earlier aphorism will cast a shadow over a later one. Or vice versa. Sometimes one fragment will throw another into relief, making of the declarative a question. Questioning how it is that the declarative could not have known itself as a question rather than a statement. And sometimes what is cast as a question is, in truth, an act of dissembling. The question, it turns out, is ontologically sure of itself, only masquerading as a question.

Sometimes the prefiguring contained within the aphorism finds its fulfillment. Sometimes it seems constitutively incomplete, as if in need of further elucidation.

Similarly, in the writing, the aphorisms or fragments sometimes appeared ready to present themselves, without provocation, without the thinking of another. In other instances, however, the aphorism or the fragment could only be uncovered through the thinking of another—say, the work of a Wendy Brown or the call to arms of a Patrick Henry. In still other instances, it required a Jay Fliegelman's attention to the performative language of the Declaration of Independence and Bill of Rights to reveal how the thinking of a Thomas Jefferson or a James Madison is awash in the discourse of grievance. Finally, in other instances, only an unexpected detour through Slavoj Žižek's critique of liberal democracy offered a thinking of grievance.

This drawing on from within and from without, then, points to a contradiction that sustained the writing. For all the concatenation between aphorism and fragment, among aphorisms and among fragments, both aphorism and fragment insist upon themselves as independent articulations. Capable of standing alone. Not reliant upon anything other than what it is they, individually, assert— or draw into question. As if, contra Jaspers, that could say "everything at once." As if it were a priori self-sufficient, its contraction no impediment to its self-sufficiency, containing within itself everything of worth that there is to be said about grievance. And yet not. The insights provided by, say, Jefferson remind us of the contradiction between that which can be said to reveal itself autochthonously and that which requires the thinking of the other so that it can come into writing and, in so doing, into itself.

This is the form, identifiably its own, in which *Grievance* insisted it be written. That form in which brevity is no obstacle to the proclamation of the aphorism as a complete truth, in which the aphorism and the fragment reinforce, illuminate, and contradict each other, and draw each other into question.

In that form the whole constitutes a mode of thinking grievance that could not be achieved through the encounter with only the aphorism or the fragment. It may also be that the whole both exceeds the sum of its parts and, more provocatively, threatens always to explode the aphorisms and fragments out of both their singularity and their imagined coherence.

Sometimes the form itself is the first marker of how the precarity that is thinking grievance manifests itself. Writing grievance may very well contain the seeds for a grievance against the form that writing grievance insists upon assuming.

The obstinacy of grievance. The difficulty of writing grievance in the face of such obduracy.

It might then be that the best that can be done is to acknowledge the force and veracity of Jaspers's argument. It is not possible to "say everything at once."

Writing grievance, however, will not submit to such modesty. It insists that it is possible to "say everything." And it may even be worth trying to do so "at once." Maybe even all at once, no matter the form it takes.

Acknowledgments

Writing *Grievance* was an experience I enjoyed thoroughly. That I was able to do so owes a great deal to Robert and Jeff. Over the course of almost two decades, their insights have proven consistently invaluable. Robert is possessed of a critical eye that always sees where there is work to be done. Jeff's perspicuity is unparalleled.

My thanks to Marco Abel and Roland Vegso. They were key to identifying those moments when explication was imperative. In the moment of decision, they were gracious in their understanding.

My editor, Matthew Engelke, surprised me with his enthusiasm for the project. I am grateful for the latitude he allowed me.

Jean-Paul Martinon probed, presenting me with, as is his wont, difficulties of the highest order. I offer this acknowledgment entirely sure that I have addressed his critiques only insufficiently.

Ron Juffer left me a bequest most cruel: a love for playing golf, a game for which I have no aptitude.

I miss playing with you, Grandad.

Aphorisms I
Grievance
On Names and Time

The Declaration's preamble interests us more than its list of grievances.

—Garry Wills, *Inventing America: Jefferson's Declaration of Independence*

I.

Grievance is more American than apple pie.

II.

America is a nation founded in grievance.

To know this, we need only forgo the poetry of Jefferson's Preamble and focus our attention solely on the prose of grievance.

III.

The Declaration of Independence lists twenty-seven articles of grievance.

It says something of grievance then that Jefferson considered the Declaration the first presentation of the American mind to the world.

IV.

America is a nation temporarily sundered by grievance (1861–1865).

America is a nation brought into global disrepute by the events of January 6, 2021.

On January 6, America revealed the depth and resilience of its grievance to the world, again. 1776. 1861. 2021.

V.

If we look closely, how much can the preamble really hide the truth of the American self?

What kind of mind dedicates itself to pursuing happiness through grievance?

VI.

The nature of the American mind is that it compels us attend to grievance.

It is through grievance that America sets out on the road to redress.

Do not the aggrieved deserve redress? Indeed they do. Everyone should be allowed to enjoy turkey and pumpkin pie with their genocide.

Are some aggrieved not more deserving than others? Turkey and pumpkin pie.

VII.

Is it not Jefferson's consciousness of the less deserving that caused him to omit the grievance about slavery from the Declaration?

Jefferson and the House of Burgesses feared slave rebellions.

Did Jefferson fear the later rebellion of his own undeserving?

Did Jefferson think himself responsible for grievances of the undeserving aggrieved?

Good King George III, always keen to foment an uprising when it suited his purposes, was eager to encourage slave rebellions.

VIII.

John Lind, graduate of Balliol College, barrister, Oxford University, philandering priest, tutor to a Polish prince.

Critic of the American Revolution.

He saw the Declaration's hypocrisy clearly.

He mocked Jefferson, a faux "assertor of liberty."

Jefferson sought redress only for himself and his kind.

IX.

In grievance that America achieves its ipseity: its selfness of self.

Grievance is America's ipseity.

A perjured ipseity faithful to its aggrieved self.

A self that turns toward grievance because it cannot turn away from itself, because it will not face itself.

America is a self, divided internally, into parts unequal.

Incompossibility: the enduring contradiction between these unequal but mutually constituting selves.

America is a nation that does not need to ask itself if there might be one true self.

America already holds the truth of grievance to be self-evident, refusing absolutely to venture beyond this truth.

In this truth, comfort.

America: One Nation, Indivisible.

America: Mission Incompossible.

X.

In the Civil War white America showed itself a nation true to grievance.

A war that some constituencies in the aggrieved South, militarily defeated but ideologically unbowed, contrived to find a new name for: "The War Between the States."

A war the South fought to ensure their states' rights.

Shelby Foote, Mississippi native and much venerated Civil War historian, is of the opinion that "there is some justice to the claim that slavery was overemphasized."[1] Not justification but "justice."

Out of that "justice," the incendiary promise—the irrepressible threat—that "the South will rise again."

Not the American Civil War. A war between independent nations.

A second war of—for—independence. A war against Yankee aggression.

The aggrieved South, bitter still today, angry at the injustice that was the Union Army's numerical and technological superiority over their Confederates.

Outnumbered, outgunned. Before the Civil War was even over, Texan Confederates were sweeping westward, doing all they could to cleanse the land before them of the indigenous. In California, the Gold Rush—among other things—drastically reduced the native population.

The antebellum South: not defeated but oppressed.

The Civil War was not lost in Mississippi. We are simply living through an extended "cessation in hostilities."

Grievance contracted into and elevated to the status of proper nouns: Shiloh, Gettysburg.

And, worst of all, Appomattox. The name of defeat. Thirteen days, March 29 to April 9, 1865. Robert E. Lee put to the sword by Ulysses S. Grant.

Appomattox: the unpalatable name of the South's surrender.

Appomattox: how grievance constructs itself as a language in which nouns rule. In which the noun bears the most powerful evocation. It is enough to say "Ap-po-mat-tox."

Four syllables. It takes no more.

So it is that grievance proclaims itself in the always-living memory that is "Robert E. Lee."

In the poetry of Robbie Robertson of The Band fame:

> Back with my wife in Tennessee
> When one day she called to me
> "Virgil, quick, come see
> There goes Robert E. Lee!"
> Now, I don't mind chopping wood
> And I don't care if the money's no good
> You take what you need
> And you leave the rest
> But they should never
> Have taken the very best[2]

VIII.

Because he was the "very best," Robert E. Lee can never truly have been "taken," taken away, lost to history. Lee endures, no matter the Confederate statues taken down in the South. The phantasm that is the transcendent Lee sees more than just the destruction visited upon his vision of the South.

Lee, his spirit still permeating those loyal to the Lost Cause, remains visible to those who would today gladly take up arms with him.

Who knows, if faith is kept in Lee's spirit, it may very well be that the best of the "very best" is yet to come.

But only if there is fidelity to grievance. If the aggrieved keep the memory of injustice alive. Nurture it, in a Jeffersonian spirit: "The tree of liberty must be refreshed from time to time with the blood of patriots and tyrants. It is its natural manure."

Provided, of course, that we acknowledge Jefferson's debt to Tertullian, one of the fathers of the early Christian church. Based in Carthage, this African church father, fully immersed in the logic of the Resurrection, proclaimed, "The blood of the martyrs is the seed of the church."[3] The event of the Resurrection must reproduce itself, as often as is needed, in miniature. And it must do so with no less commitment to Jesus-the-Christ's sacrifice.

Does the "tree of liberty" offer shade and rhetorical cover to both "patriots and tyrants"? And if the tree has foliage enough to cover both, is it not likely that one will become indistinct from the other? If they conduct their battle beneath this potentially ample foliage, will not their blood commingle? Are we not then to expect a consanguinity between "patriot and tyrant"?

XI.

Do patriot and tyrant become one in Jefferson; Washington; Adams, John and Samuel; and Patrick Henry?

XII.

We should be suspicious of these blood ties. In no small measure because the "tree of liberty" rhetoric

evokes the blood of martyrs logic rather than a reenactment of a revolutionary call to arms. Unlike the 1776 revolutionaries, the 2021 insurrectionists wanted only to stage a martyr-like act in order to recall past, actual martyrs.

Not all martyrs are equal.

The 2021 shaman's body paint is not the blood of a martyr. It is political theater, enacted for spectacular public consumption and, as such, worthy only of condemnation.

Showmanship, or, more simply, shamanship.

The fake remains inauthentic, especially when it comes in such theatrical attire—or lack thereof.

Not even all faux martyrs are equal.

Not even when they multiply themselves four times over. Claim different names.

"QAnon Shaman," "Jacob Chansley," "Jake Angeli," and, in keeping with the theme of bestiality, the "Yellowstone Wolf."

Patrick Henry wore a shirt. That's the bare minimum dress code for a revolutionary.

Come properly attired.

Making an economic exception, of course, for the French Revolution's sans culottes. They came dressed, those foot soldiers of the French Revolution, as best they could.

Barely dressed.

That was their revolutionary attire.

Needs must: come as you are.

XIII.

Worth a moment's pause. A pause that we might think the spirit of Jefferson as he wrote the Declaration, as Garry Wills suggests: "The best way to honor the spirit of Jefferson is to use his doubting intelligence again on his own text. Only skepticism can save him from his devotees, return us to the drier air of his scientific maxims, all drawn with the same precision that went into his architectural sketches."[4]

The organizational name that follows Lee, condensed into repetition. A hard consonant.

Biblical in its evocation: a trinity of Ks.

XIV.

As we might see at a baseball game.

The number of strikeouts achieved by a pitcher.

Jarring, so conceived.

Ominous, this seeing three Ks in the stands at a ball game.

Drawing us up short.

Thrusting us back into history: 1947.

Strike I! K.

Baseball: Segregation: Jackie Robinson: the Brooklyn Dodgers.

Vociferous white opposition to integration.

Teammates, opposing players, opposing managers, fans, on both sides, free to give vent.

They voice their grievance, loudly.

They are aggrieved by his intrusion.

Into what is theirs.

Baseball, it's a white man's game.

Strike II! KK.

Robinson, the target of white hatred.

On the field and off it.

Robinson is told he can play their game only if he can encase his volatile temper in lead.

The Negro who integrates is denied his right to be aggrieved. Who dares speak against Thanksgiving?

To act against those who are aggrieved.

That is the price of admission.

He must endure. In silence.

Are you strong enough *not* to fight back?

Baseball, as American as.

Grievance, more American,

than baseball.

Strike III! KKK

XV.

The organizational name that arose out of defeat, out of the consciousness of a degradation unbearable to white America, an organizational name born out of hostility to the unfulfilled promise that was Reconstruction, an organizational name that played its part in putting paid to the promise of Reconstruction. KKK: the name determined to stand fast against the intolerable prospect of slave now made equal with the master.

Nathan Bedford Forrest. Defeated Civil War veteran, founder of the KKK. Bedford Forrest saw in Confederate defeat the need to keep fighting the battle to maintain America as a nation ruled only by white men. By any means necessary. Bedford Forrest saw how easy it was to swap the gray rags of the Confederacy for the white robes of racial supremacy. He knew how to rearm in the cause of the never-to-be-Lost Cause.

White American Grievance, clad in all white. *Sheeeet*.

Grievance, undisguised into unconstrained violence; undisguised in its disguise.

A little like the secret, grievance. The secret is not that which is unknown. It is that which is known but presented as an unknown. The secret is, instead, an item, a scrap, or even a body of knowledge to which we are all privy.

XVI.

For the aggrieved, its actions never rise to the level of Nietzschean revenge. The actions of the aggrieved are always the actions of the just. *Iusta de causa. Causa damnata est iusta causa.* Always.

In *Zarathustra* Friedrich Nietzsche seeks a means of breaking the never-ending cycle of revenge.

The aggrieved never offend. It always claims for itself the status of the offended.

Grievance is beholden only to its own unimpugnable logic.

Grievance is the gift that keeps on giving.

XVII.

To proclaim the aggrieved self true to grievance is to do more than (what it means when the aggrieved) pledge fidelity to grievance. It is to know what it means for the aggrieved to be faithful to grievance and to insist upon the grievance in question as a priori true.

To know what it means for the aggrieved to appropriate for grievance the status of truth indubitably, thereby putting paid to any notion that draws the truth of grievance into doubt.

It is to make the self's grievance unimpugnable to the other. *Thanksgiving.*

XVIII.

The truth of grievance as inauthentic, but assertively so. The inauthentic overwhelms its inauthenticity through repeatedly and aggressively declaring itself true.

XIX.

That which grievance takes to be true is, in being so proclaimed, made truth. The effect of this appropriation is to make of fidelity or truth a loyalty to grievance. If the aggrieved self is faithful to truth, the aggrieved self must then be loyal to grievance.

XX.

Today inauthentic truth goes by many names, one of which is salient only because it is so entirely lacking in irony. Without fear of contradiction, to say nothing of its inherent self-contradiction, it proclaims itself the bearer of "alternative facts."

XXI.

If we are to follow this logic, can we then say that friendship or love, each in its own way an instance of fidelity, can be construed as a loyalty to grievance?

XXII.

The aggrieved is never *a* subject. It is always *the* subject.

Grievance is a mode of subjectivation. Cast out by

history, it is the mode through which the aggrieved constitutes itself as a subject against history. The aggrieved constitutes itself as that subject committed to keeping the temporal impropriety that is history in check.

XXIII.

Ahistory. A history for all time that is without time.

Ahistory today, ahistory tomorrow, ahistory forever.

Ahistory is a false *physis*. Ahistory proclaims itself that time when there is absolute coinciding between a self that has a monopoly on power and a self that has subdued nature.

Nature is made to conform to the power of the unaggrieved self.

The self only becomes aggrieved when the harmony between power and nature is disturbed.

In ahistory there is no opposition between physis and nomos.

Ahistory is the state of unaggrieved idyll.

Ahistory is a state of being that is always on the verge of being lost.

To history.

By history.

History, that state in which *physis* and *nomos* consider themselves free to be in conflict.

No order on the order of ahistory.

Every nature free to manifest itself, in the order of its choosing.

Time, the agent of history. Time, how history intrudes upon, disrupts the order of ahistory.

XXIV.

The subject of ahistory seeks not subjectivation but de-subjectivation.

It strives for the anonymity, the inveterate sameness of self that only ahistory can guarantee.

Subjectivation marks the failure of ahistory, thereby necessitating de-subjectivation.

The aggrieved desire only to be distinguishable among their own in their ahistory.

And distinguishable, absolutely, from the other.

XXV.

Grievance, for the aggrieved, calls upon the aggrieved subject to reconstitute itself.

To reconstitute itself once more. Grievance reconstitutes as the newly aggrieved self.

As unaggrieved. Once more. To restore the harmony between *physis* and *nomos*.

The aggrieved subject reconstitutes itself, again and again, toward that harmonious end.

Specifically aggrieved, and yet not. The lack of specificity resides, of course, in the fact that all aggrieved selves are constituted in terms recognizable to each other. Maybe even recognizable as each other.

Each moment constitutes an ontology of the present-past.

Each reconstitution a guarding against the loss of ahistory.

Ahistory, the ultimate prophylactic against history.

XXVI.

The act of the aggrieved always takes as its pretext and governing rationale the existential threat that the other poses to the Republic.

The Revolutionary War established the Republic.

The other threatened its existence in 1861.

As did Reconstruction.

As did the civil rights movement.

As did a 2020 defeat in the presidential election.

XXVII.

In other words, the aggrieved cannot be held responsible for their actions. For the actions undertaken in the cause of redressing grievance. Such as overthrowing a tyrannical monarch or proclaiming the right of Southern states to secede so that they could continue to practice slavery.

For the aggrieved the attribution of responsibility is a tricky business.

It can, especially under epoch-defining circumstances, be claimed. Or it can, under more contentious circumstances, be displaced.

A little like Alexander Hamilton's definition of responsibility in the Federalist Papers. Best phrased as: history made me do it.

Its most muscular revolutionary articulation is, of course, Patrick Henry's "Give me liberty, or give me death!"

A noble sentiment. It holds out the possibility of transcendence: liberty can be found, if not in life, then in death. A life given over to death when the aggrieved gives itself over to a just cause. Revolution made the symptomatic Patrick Henry do it—die, metaphorically, for the Revolution. Or, in the justifiable terms of the Declaration, George III made the symptomatic Patrick Henry do it.

The effect of Patrick Henry's justification marks him at once as first among the aggrieved. It makes him distinct from the likes of Nathan Bedford Forrest and the January 6 insurrectionists.

Not all grievance is equal. Nor do all the aggrieved occupy the same plane of grievance. Some grievances are more equal than others.[5]

"George III made me do it" is not *the same as a shaman-clad insurrectionist declaring, on January 6, 2021, something on the order of, "The 'stolen election' made me do it." Or another, assuming the guise of "Yellowstone Wolf," offering the defense of lycanthropy. As if Jacob Chansley were, between name changes, a keen Renaissance scholar with an especial interest in John Webster's* The Duchess of Malfi. *On January 6, the US Capitol was stormed in the name of grievance.*

What they have in common is their recurrence, without denying the importance of difference, across the expanse of American history. How they recur, most often with echoes of each other; how it is they sometimes consider themselves at liberty to invoke each other, as if one can provide absolute cover for the other.

XXVIII.

It is their inequality that we must keep hold of if we are to keep their difference in full view. It is not enough to proclaim difference. It matters more that difference is constantly, rigorously thought. Insisted upon as a matter for thinking.

XXII.

We must think grievance so that we can grasp it more fully when we find ourselves confronted with a signal difficulty—as in the distinction between Patrick

Henry and the January 6 insurrectionists. How is the thinking of grievance as a philosophical concept and as a repeating political problem be understood as separate from, say, the *ressentiment*-laden depthless morass that so defines our moment? Is such a distinction even possible? Or should we simply face things as they appear to be and acknowledge that the *ressentiment*-laden muck that presents itself so routinely is but a step away from grievance as we are endeavoring to conceptualize it? How is it that grievance can so stubbornly retain its viability as a concept?

XXIX.

And yet we know that whatever its viability as a concept, however it appears to border, perilously, upon other similar concepts, our path to thinking grievance, however we conceive of or name it, must find its way through grievance.

It may be the only place from which we can undertake our work.

And, given its recurrence, there could surely be no better place to begin than that mode of being-toward-the-other in which America presents its core to us.

Grievance, more American than apple pie.

Grievance, out of which America begins. Does its persistence mean that America is a nation that will end in grievance? Because of grievance?

"Grievance thou art, and unto grievance thou shalt return."

According to G. K. Chesterton, that would be the only appropriate end. Chesterton found the Declaration to be "dogmatic and theological."[6]

What you sow in grievance, so shall you reap.

The January 6 insurrectionists as the spoiled, contaminated fruit of that thinking that procured the victory of 1776.

XXX.

But is spoiled fruit not better than no fruit at all?

When will the grievance of the other find redress?

Ever? Turkey and pumpkin pie.

XXXI.

Grievance is aggrieved.

It inveighs against those institutional forces that will not readily submit to it. That dare to hold it to account.

Such a call to account it names "weaponization."

Grievance erases from memory the ways institutional authority acted against the other.

Through notorious surveillance.

J. Edgar Hoover, Martin Luther King Jr.

Grievance is in no way above petty complaining.

What is good for the goose is not good for the gander.

What goes round must not come round.

That is the position of the aggrieved, and they cannot be shaken from it.

Grievance acts with the petulance of a spoiled child.

And will happily continue to do so.

Ahistory is the cocoon of the indulged.

It is a cocoon that insulates the aggrieved against the demands.

The aggrieved dream of perpetual childhood.

The sustaining dream of the aggrieved is a life lived in the safety of the cocoon.

The aggrieved see no reason to enter the turbulent waters of history.

They are afraid that they might be overwhelmed.

The aggrieved would rather die aggrieved than give up the delusion that is ahistory.

The aggrieved know death as a hydra-headed prospect spawned and nurtured by grievance.

So intimate with death are the aggrieved that they are moved to make themselves its instrument.

By making themselves its instrument, the aggrieved are convinced that they will die last.

To die last, that is the ultimate victory of which the aggrieved dream.

He who dies last wins. Maybe. Only sometimes.

A victory, yes, but a tragic one.

Who will know that the aggrieved died last?

Who is left to salute the victory of the aggrieved?

Who remains to offer obeisance when all others are dead?

Who dreams of playing this game named the unchanging same for all time?

Who will speak against cheating?

Why cheat when you have already won?

Can the aggrieved live without grievance?

Will the aggrieved die railing that they have been deprived of grievance?

Against whom will the aggrieved shake its fist in anger?

Is there no justice in the world for the aggrieved?

Is their dream always to be thwarted?

Must history always win?

XXXII.

What a perniciously patient force is history.

History wins simply by waiting things out.

History, thy name is Godot.

Godot, the high priest of patience.

Invincible.

The aggrieved are no match for Godot's long-suffering army.

That wins by waiting.

Godot's army shows us that doing nothing is the only plan that guarantees victory.

Always.

We know of many encounters that testify to the sagacity of Godot's army.

Napoleon marching against Russia.

Hitler marching against Russia.

Retreat, lay waste to everything as you retreat, put your faith in winter, and then do nothing.

Now is the winter of our great content.

Just wait.

Wait and win.

If it is not the meek who will inherit the earth, then it will most certainly be the patient.

Waiting requires no heroes because it actively dislikes heroes.

Heroes cannot stop themselves. They are predisposed to do.

They rage, heroes.

XXXIII.

The work of grievance is to set right that which the other has made unnatural—the other's determination to undo the present-past.

Grievance, so understood, is the restoration of the natural order of things.

XXXIV.

The only way grievance can restore the natural order of things to naturalize defiance.

To do so grievance seeks recourse to Natural Right—the inalienable right of the aggrieved—which for grievance is superior to human law.

Human law is inherently unjust in its refusal to accede to the terms of Natural Right. This is the truth that grievance holds as most "self-evident."

XXXV.

This is the truth that grievance of ahistory "must have been dreaming about all along."[7]

To dream the sweet dream of insurrection. It is with the dream of ahistory as an infinitely sustainable time that the aggrieved arms itself.

This is the dream first imbibed with mother's milk.

With the white mother's white milk.

The aggrieved must have had it in their heads all along, this inalienable right to grievance, this right to act as they see fit, given to them by ahistory.

The right to act aggrieved is the stuff of every school-child's dream.

Every white schoolchild's dream.

XXXVI.

"It is a fine thing," writes the Czech poet Miroslav Holub, "that boys have heads."

So that they can dream, their heads always turned to and filled with grievance.

Are there no other dreams that these boys, proud, defiant, comrades-in-grievance, militantly white, can dream?

Is there no dream that enters their heads that does not involve violence against the other? Why do these dreams always have a nightmarish element? Do these boys only dream darkly, that is, do they only dream of death?

Grievance makes them heady.

XXXVII.

Or maybe George III inspired these dreams when he "excited domestic insurrection among us, & has endeavored to bring on the inhabitants of our frontiers the merciless Indian savages, whose known rules of warfare is an undistinguished destruction of all ages, sexes & conditions."[8]

In a nation founded upon grievance, the other is a "merciless Indian savage." Made into a tool of injustice.

The frontier belongs to its rightful "inhabitants."

The other provokes the aggrieved to "domestic insurrection."

Over two and a half centuries, domestic insurrection has shown itself to have many faces.

Sometimes that face is terrifying-comedic.

A face that does not rise to the status of tragic.

A face only the king of grievance could love.

Self-love, thy name is Grievance.

A face that knows how to peddle grievance.

A face that is now accompanied by a number: PO 1135809.

Grievance assumes the aspect of a common criminal.

Isn't the grievance of ahistory always first cousin to crime?

With its number, grievance has the kind of face that makes you want to laugh.

And look at it in horror.

And wonder how grievance can come to assume such a lurid face.

The pose is intended to be menacing.

That it is, rather, an etching in the bitterness of the aggrieved surprises us not one jot.

Except that the aggrieved of ahistory see in such a face not bitterness but he who "excited domestic insurrection among us."

With justifiable cause, the aggrieved bellow, as if priming themselves for further domestic unrest.

Every insurrection contains within itself a harbinger of the one to come.

Every insurrection is an avatar—the next one will descend from it.

As it has been from the beginning.

XXXVIII.

Because it assumes a set of rights and declares itself free to dream these dreams of destruction, grievance takes as its first and enduring articulation the unarguable truth of difference.

This dream, these rights, are an exclusive preserve.

These dreams, these rights, begin with that first iteration of difference: the Declaration.

A difference that presumed many other differences.

The Declaration made Americans a nation distinct from their British colonial rulers. It ruptured Americans from their European forbears. And yet it did not.

Revolutionary Americans and their heirs are made distinct by their desire for sovereignty—"One nation, under God." No matter, America's is a sovereignty still mightily entangled with the politics, culture, and economy of Britain and Europe.

Independence could not, even in its most strident articulation, either overcome (at least not completely) or overwhelm (by erasing all traces of Britain and Europe) the fact of consanguinity.

XXXIX.

"We hold these truths to be self-evident, that all men are created equal…"

All except the indigenous people and the slaves. These populations were distinct and had to be kept apart from all the other "men created equal."

These populations were irredeemably different.

Jefferson names blackness an "immovable evil."

Sally Hemmings.

Elided grievance.

Hypocrisy.

One of America's great gifts to the world.

Count Jefferson, esteemed scribe of liberty, among the greatest of this sort.

The right to grievance, then, could never extend to the constitutively unequal. It cannot extend to this other, no doubt because of the other's propensity for "immovable evil." Either that, or perhaps the other's right to grievance was denied on the grounds of "savagery," of having no "civilization."

Possessed of not even a shamanistic civilization.

XL.
The savage's threat to the aggrieved must be declared at the nation's founding.

The savage and its ilk are what the aggrieved will have to overcome.

Again and again.

XLI.
A shamanistic civilization that is warrior-like, daubed red-white-blue. A face ready to do battle.

To fight for its rights.

That will never give up the fight.

This warrior spirit is what the other so patently lacks.

The other does not know how to summon up such a spirit of resistance.

The other does not know how to access its warrior spirit of old.

The other has succumbed to modernity. Has been enfeebled by modernity. Made soft by technology. The other's warrior muscles have atrophied.

Only the shaman can revive that spirit of old.

XLII.

The shaman is the face of difference.

Unrecognizable to the other.

What knows the other of going into battle with a painted face?

The other can no longer do battle armed only with a spear.

The other does not dare to reinvigorate its autochthonous, primeval self.

Only the aggrieved of ahistory can summon up such a being. Make it live again.

Make it live again as the irrepressible spirit of ahistory.

Vengeful, this spirit, but not without a performative demeanor too.

This spirit knows how to erupt into history out of the confines of ahistory.

It is possessed of a transcendence that allows it to impress itself on more than one season, this spirit, this tricolor-faced shaman. Who is not a merciless Indian.

It will intrude where it sees fit, this spear-bearing shaman.

Hail to the shaman.

XLIII.

It is brave. As those who are buttressed by the like-minded insurrectionists are brave.

A bravery all its own.

A bravery that makes the shaman stand out in the crowd.

The shaman never asks if it could only stand safely so surrounded. It never asks if its safety derives entirely from being in the company of its insurrectionist fellows; fellows who have not yet ascended to so advanced a stage of aggrieved being.

The face of the aggrieved must mark itself as different, showing the shamanistic face of the aggrieved to the world.

Even if that difference is only warrior paint deep.

Insurrection, the shaman reminds us, is the first refuge of the scoundrel.

XLIV.

Shaman, be not afraid to assert your untrue self.

Take, as you must, liberties with the truth.

Seeking redress for your grievances is your inalienable right.

Does not democracy, hallowed by a constitution, follow insurrection?

Who cares for amendments, especially as they

proceed from 13?

Is 13 not an unlucky number?

Were 12 amendments not enough?

What are 13, 14, and 15 if not a rebuke to the irreproachable Founding Fathers?

XLV.

Do you not, shaman, like Jefferson and Lee, take comfort in the knowledge that it is only in insurrection that you can find your happiness?

Are they not, these patriots of yore, close kin?

Only in insurrection can you find again your affinity with the Fathers of Revolution and the denizens of unresolved civil strife.

The work of insurrection is never done.

Rise, shaman, rise.

Your time has come.

Once more.

Jefferson, thou nimble, artful dodger.

Irrepressible, you, Jefferson.

So it is that we always find our way back to you, master of the quill.

Does all American writing derive from Monticello?

Is that where all American writing points?

Virginia is for writers.

Of grand documents that proceed by sleight of racial hand.

Of white hands that embrace black bodies but elide them in writing.

Of white hands that love black bodies but permit them no place in the body politic.

Of a white love that speaks its name.

Posthumously.

XLVI.

The case is not *Loving v Virginia*.

Love bears no counterpoint.

One way or another, there has always been love for whites in Virginia.

XLVII.

It is always of Jefferson that America writes.

Forget Poe and his purloined letter. Jefferson is the American writer who must always be addressed.

In love and lore, in love and law, in lore and law, America finds its echo in Jefferson.

Aphorisms II
Grief

I.

Grief, as in the loss of a loved one, is the price we pay for love.

Grief knows love as a singular, unconvertible currency.

II.

Grief knows love as a loss and as an excess.

Grief knows what it means to love, to love too much. To reprimand the self for having loved not enough.

Grief knows the devastation that only the loss of love, of a loved one, of the beloved, can effect.

Grief knows the substance and superficiality of affect.

Grief knows the importance and the senselessness of mourning.

Sometimes grief makes you keep the wrong company.

Even knowing this, grief insists that bad company is better than no company at all.

Sometimes it is hard to tell grief from misery.

III.

Grief accepts, much as it resists, the irretrievability that is loss.

That is why grief struggles so determinedly against such irretrievability. Grief is imbued with the spirit of Sisyphus.

Grief lives fully aware of the loss it has incurred. This loss cannot be overcome.

IV.

Grief knows time at once, by turns, as friend and enemy.

V.

Grief opens itself to the contingency that is time. Grief knows that it is at the mercy of time. That time can surprise, that time can inflict further harm.

Grief knows that it clings in vain to the aphorism, "Time heals all wounds." Grief knows the truth.

Time heals nothing at all. Grief knows time as a seducer. Time lulls those who grieve into a false forgetting. It is a forgetting made permeable by the force that is remembering, remembering that time inscribed with grief. Time as living-with-in grief.

Grief's intimacy with time makes it wary of the aphoristic. Grief knows that loss cannot be contracted into a pithiness. Grief demands its own vocabulary, one as poignant as it is flexible, as open to living with trauma as it to the recollection of love. Grief abides the painful proximity of happiness and loss, much as it chafes against, resents, even, that proximity. Thinks the proximity a cruelty.

Grief knows that loss will present itself again. Time knows grief as a constant companion, unshakeable, in the face of everything.

VI.

Grief understands that loss cannot and must not, ever, be overcome.

Grief knows that there is love in loss.

Grief ponders the possibility that it might know loss without love. And in its contemplation, grief comes to embrace the love that loss, and loss alone, maybe, can animate.

Grief knows that it has within itself the capacity to bring to life love through loss.

Grief can teach the self to love, can set the self on the road to love. To love what it did not know it could love.

Grief wonders at its own limits. Can it teach the self to love that which it does not love but which lives?

Grief, in its modesty, proffers no answers. It prefers, sometimes, to work only by way of the interrogative. Grief asks, Can this be loved? Not satisfied, it persists: Can this be loved now? At its most insistent, it wants to know why the self resists loving this now. Grief warns against loving too late.

Grief has no patience with the latent J. Alfred Prufrock we each harbor within us. That spindly man incapacitated by a grief that has already, unbeknownst to Prufrock, overwhelmed him into ennui.

Grief has no appetite for a man who would not simply eat a peach. It does not tarry with a man rendered inert because what matters to him is whether his trousers are turned; or not, as fashion dictates.

VII.
Grievance is not grief.

VIII.
Grief becomes grievance at that moment when the self submits to the logic of extraction. When the self decides that its loss can only be endured if

something—say, retribution—or someone—the other in one guise or another—is made villainous.

IX.

Grief can be made into grievance through the law.

The law is how grievance comes to overcome grief.

America is, it is said, a litigious society.

Grief allows for mourning. Grief would rather not be subject to the unpredictability that emerges out of loss. But grief makes accommodation for the various instantiations that loss might take, for the recurrence of loss in moments least expected. Grief commits itself to the struggle with memory. Grievance demands compensation. Grievance insists upon restitution.

X.

Grievance is devoid of humor. Grievance refuses to reflect upon itself unless such self-reflection can validate the self's grievance. Grievance asks no questions. Grievance asserts. Asserts again. And again.

Grievance is always on the verge of being angry with history—at least that history that does not affirm its injury.

XI.

Grievance always misses the joke.

This makes grievance unable to understand Robbie Robertson's wry response to the joke that history played on him. The son of an indigenous Canadian woman, Robertson only found out when he was thirteen that the man who raised him, James Robertson, was not his biological father. He was, instead, the son of a Jewish man who had died before his mother married James Robertson.

"You could say I'm an expert when it comes to persecution."

The joke is capacious. Capricious, it can abide within itself loss, love, pain, historical acuity, and pathos. Alive within the joke is longing for that which was not known as well as for that which was not known because it cannot be known.

Inside the joke is a deep reservoir of intuition.

The joke does not declaim because it is confident that it can pass over the scabrous, the historically unspeakable, as a thing that must be parsed with a smile.

The joke knows its own power.

Grievance, on the other hand, seeks only to own— monopolize—power. For its own purposes. The joke, which so often bears on death, knows enough to share itself with the world.

Grievance wants to keep the world in check.

XII.

In this respect, grievance has good instincts. Grievance is not for sharing; but the effects of grievance reach well beyond itself.

Grievance is governed by the illusory logic that is infinite self-possession.

A self-possession determined to dispossess the other.

The joke disperses itself into the world, fully aware that it can never claim ownership over itself.

Grievance suffers from that condition we might name toxic accumulation. The more grievance accrues to itself, the higher rises the toxicity quotient within it.

Left to itself, grievance might very well destroy itself.

But because grievance draws its sustenance and vitality from its proximity to the other, grievance emits its toxicity to all who approach it.

Like misery, grievance loves company. Most of the time.

XIII.

Grievance cannot, and most decidedly will not, abide loss.

Contingency cannot be permitted within the logic of grievance.

XIV.

Grief becomes grievance at that precise moment when grieving is instrumentalized into an act of retribution against the other.

An instrumentalization that is timeless because it can be reactivated. Again, when the aggrieved is made to endure an unjustifiable loss.

XV.

Grievance does not struggle with memory. It simply recalls, reactivates, reanimates, recalibrates. Memory is made into a potent weapon by grievance.

A memory that always has the other within its sights.

Memory lies dormant, volcanically, within the psyche of the aggrieved.

XVI.

Writing in his *Memoirs*, the victorious Union Army commander Grant reflects on his vanquished foe:

> What General Lee's feelings were I do not know. As he was a man of much dignity, with an impassible face, it was impossible to say whether he felt inwardly glad that the end had finally come, or felt sad over the result, and was too manly to show it. Whatever his feelings, they were entirely concealed from my observation; but my

own feelings, which had been quite jubi-
lant upon the receipt of his letter, were sad
and depressed. I felt like anything rather
than rejoicing at the downfall of a foe who
had fought so long and valiantly, and had
suffered so much for a cause, though that
cause was, I believe, one of the worst for
which a people ever fought, and one for
which there was the least excuse.[9]

Grant, however highly he regards his former Union comrade, no matter that Lee "fought so long and valiantly," is clear in his distaste for the cause Lee served. Grant will have no truck with Lee's cause, "one of the worst for which a people ever fought."

Still, Grant cannot help but find himself taken with the inscrutability of Lee's visage. How, after all, is one to discern a man's innermost feelings when he possesses such an "impassible face"?

Grant wants to know what thoughts, and, more importantly, what "feelings" are denied him by Lee's "dignified" stoicism.

It is the loss of access to what it is Lee thinks that preoccupies Grant most.

XVII.

Is Lee's the face of "dignified grief"?

Or, as seems more likely, is Grant's desire for

explication itself but another face of grief?

Or, as seems even more likely, is this how grief looks on grief? And yet cannot, like forbidden love, bring itself to name grief "grief"?

Is grief the most incomprehensible of all affects? The most inaccessible of affects? The most poorly tolerated by human beings? The most stubbornly obtuse? The most sovereign, imperious, and superior of all affects?

Is that why the grief Lee evokes in Grant not only grief but also human empathy?

XVIII.

"From suffering can come empathy."[10]

Does empathy make it possible to ameliorate the other's suffering? What does empathy make the empathizer do? Does empathy demand anything in relation to the suffering? Does it matter who caused the suffering of the other? Is the empathizer only responsible for the suffering that the self inflicted upon the other? Can we imagine an empathy that *is*? That is, simply in and of itself. An empathy that responds, regardless. Is an empathy that is specifically self-oriented and not inclined toward universality, even empathy?

Aphorisms III
Achilles:
Grievance, Grief, Love

I.

It is the belligerence makes them unforgettable. That is why we remember their names.

We forget Priam; we remember Achilles.

He is a man of vengeance, Achilles.

So much so that even his vanquished dead foes are not spared.

Day after day, Hector must be killed.

Achilles makes Hector live.

In the name of Patroclus.

Achilles stands first in the pantheon of the insatiability of grievance.

Patroclus is dead, remains dead.

And with every new death that Achilles visits upon Hector, he condemns Patroclus to be second in death.

To come after the one who killed him.

How the aggrieved know not their victory.

How remarkable they are, gifted in the art of snatching defeat from the jaws of victory.

Can it be said that the aggrieved know not how to be in the wake of victory?

Except that they are sure that they must put themselves once more at the disposal of death.

II.

All aggrieved being is being toward death.

It may be that it is only in being toward death that they feel themselves on solid ground.

But beneath their feet, the earth is rumbling.

And knowing this, taking comfort in it, the aggrieved feel a quiet ecstasy course through them.

In this turbulence, with death always close, the aggrieved find themselves able to exhale.

The aggrieved affirm their existence most assertively when they are alive to the truth that their next breath might be their last.

Why waste such exhilaration on dragging Hector's body across the stony ground when he is already dead and will be restored to wholeness by the gods when Achilles returns the body at night?

This restoration to wholeness by the interfering gods infuriates Achilles.

It is as if the gods were mocking Achilles's very best efforts at disfiguring and desecrating Hector.

Mocking him in his futility.

Cruel, these gods, cruel.

Can a loyal friend not visit death upon the enemy repeatedly?

Achilles rages.

How can the gods possibly know that putting the other to death is a full-time commitment by the aggrieved?

That the aggrieved never tire of making dead the already dead?

Do the gods not know that he who dies last is not always the winner?

III.

The tirelessness of the aggrieved is a thing beyond the gods' comprehension.

Do the gods not know that grievance passeth all understanding?

Should not they, as gods, know this? How can they

claim to be gods if the insatiability and voracity grievance offends them?

What manner of gods are they?

IV.

It is only in their indefatigability that the aggrieved can manifest their love.

That they speak in the name of endurance is for them the surest sign that they are felicitous beyond measure.

The gods, it would appear, are closer in their ability to understand the ways of death to mere mortals like Priam.

It must be the rarefied air of Mount Olympus that deprives the gods of their wisdom.

How is it that, looking down on the world from such lofty heights, the gods can see things no more clearly than Priam, who watches the desecration of his son's body from a balcony?

The gods, Achilles intuits, are partisans. They have taken sides against him.

In the struggle between grievance and grief, the gods have thrown in their lot with grief.

The gods have abandoned Achilles.

It is left to him to wage the war of grievance unaided.

Achilles must enact his grievance single-handedly.

He must come to his grief by a long and lonely path.

The gods, it seems to Achilles, would rather weep with the father of Hector than bestow their favor on the warrior who wages war on a single dead body, day after day.

Is Achilles's cause not just?

What kind of creatures are these gods who turn from a soldier so brave and noble?

How could the gods choose Priam over Achilles, Hector over Patroclus?

Who would follow gods such as these?

Achilles, already knowing the manner of his death, entrusts to himself—and to himself only—the work of making dead.

V.

Until the dead are dead, once and for all, Achilles will not rest.

He has assigned himself a task, a task without end, and he will not shrink from it.

In Achilles's making dead the dead, we are introduced to the majesty of grievance.

There is nothing to do but look on his grievance with reverence.

Achilles makes of grievance a tragedy upon which we can look with favor.

Not even the dead can halt the aggrieved in the execution of their duty.

Not even the dead are safe from the diligence of the aggrieved.

In fact, it is by making dead the dead that the aggrieved reaffirm their commitment to making dead.

What Priam takes to be fanaticism, however, is an act that belongs to a higher order of things.

Day after day, Achilles is teaching himself how to grieve.

Grief if not learned simply by putting to death the warrior who killed your best friend.

Certainly not once.

VI.

With every act of making dead the dead, Achilles learns a little more of what it means to grieve.

Grieving, how to do it, this not even the gods can impute to mortals.

Only the grieving can teach themselves how to grieve.

Achilles, autodidact in the art of grieving.

Achilles, who knows that Priam is watching him making dead the dead, might be said to be instructing Priam in how to grieve.

Achilles and Priam, two Greek men learning to grieve, each holding sacred a different but inextricably linked body.

Two bodies, bound in and by death.

Is it only through the aggrieved making dead the dead that it becomes possible to know how to grieve? To know grief?

What a perverse, voracious, utterly consuming work it is, to learn grieving.

What a force is love, this love that teaches a father and a best friend to come to know grief through love.

To make dead the dead, day after day, is not to desecrate the dead, regardless of what the helpless father would have us think.

Every day, in making dead the dead, the work of grieving offers the possibility of gaining a glimpse into how it is we must incline ourselves toward the dead over whom, for whom, we grieve.

VII.

In making dead the dead, those who grieve make grief more grievable.

Achilles's is not only the fury of the friend who survives. Nor can Priam be said to be a mere helpless spectator, a father unable to protect his dead son from another public desecration.

Without Achilles's ritual desecration, Priam would not have known the innermost recesses of his love for his son.

Priam would not have come to be shocked at the capacity of grief to make us know our love in death.

Achilles's love can only find itself in making dead the dead.

Achilles, lover of Patroclus, shows grief as a mode of being toward death so singular, so completely excessive, that a new name must be appended to it.

Achilles's grief is the first that can stake a claim to the Homeric.

What a thing it is to see grief slowly, torturously slowly, fight its way out of the encampment of grievance.

To come to know grief is to break, with a violence that is entirely unprecedented, with a violence that is decisive, with a decisiveness that owes everything to violence and yet will not be held captive to violence, with the strictures of grievance.

For the aggrieved to learn grief, they must be willing to make dead.

To show the father of the dead the depth of the aggrieved's grievance, without consideration for the pain it inflicts upon the father who loved, who loves, the son.

Were grievance to dedicate itself to finding the

Homeric within itself, it might come to know the work of burrowing down into grief so deeply that the aggrieved might begin to think the fatal limits of grievance.

And find that grievance is without limit.

That grievance is grievance precisely because it is depthless, abyssal, exceeds all known boundaries.

That grievance is that concept so expansive that no thinking can contain it.

Put an end to it.

Determine where it ends.

VIII.

Grievance forecloses where it should look for ways to rupture.

Grievance seeks to reinforce where it should perforate.

Grievance is confident in itself when it should encourage doubt, when it should nurture doubt so that new ways of being toward death might present themselves.

Grievance cannot even begin to know itself unless it is willing to declare, to itself and to the world, that it possesses no mastery over itself.

Grievance must ask if it is willing to make dead grievance.

What good is grievance, this archangel of death, if it is not prepared to risk its own death?

To put itself to death by its own hand?

Of what worth is grievance if it will not rise to face itself, not as a friend, but as an enemy of its own making?

Will grievance dare to find the enemy within itself?

And what will it do if the name of that enemy reveals itself to be a genus of love so narrow and expansive, so shallow and so deep, so obvious and so incomprehensible, so accessible and so stubbornly set against self-interrogation, that grievance admits itself to be only the means and not the end?

IX.

That the end is not death but life in death.

That the architecture of grievance shows grievance to rest upon grief.

That the cocoon that houses grievance is so porous that love and grief, grief and love, penetrate it with regularity.

That grievance admits that it can never stand by itself.

And that grief alone knows sovereignty.

That grievance is always a consequence, a point of connection, inveterately dependent.

That the trace of grief can never be erased, that this

trace is always detectable.

That the more ferocious grievance is in its self-defense, the more rickety its self-construction is shown to be.

X.

Grievance may claim for itself the resilience of a spiderweb, all the while knowing that it is built out of a brittle material.

Grievance proclaims itself a truth, when it is fully aware that what it is peddling can never survive serious scrutiny.

Grievance resorts to bluster, braggadocio, and relentless self-promotion because this is the only way the confidence trick can hope to succeed.

Grievance knows that it must dazzle if it is to survive, so it assumes the appearance of a shiny object.

Grievance is well trained in the art of misdirection.

That is why it is always at risk of losing its way entirely.

Its compass is always pointed in the direction of "E": expedience.

Grievance, for this reason, is spared the fate of losing its way.

You cannot lose that which you did not know.

It is for this reason that the only proper domicile for grievance is the cocoon.

You can't really lose your way in so confined and confining a space, one of your own making, constructed according to a vision all your own.

XI.

Every day, Achilles plows the same furrow,

determined to achieve a different outcome.

That tomorrow he will not have to make dead the dead.

But because every day he fails to make dead the dead, he is left with no choice but to know that his love for Patroclus cannot be kept separate from the dead who refuse to die.

In Hector's daily reconstitution, no matter how much violence Achilles does to the body, Achilles confronts the heartbreaking limit of his grievance.

The gods, in their wisdom, demand, no matter how defiant Achilles returns every day to claim Hector's body so that he can mutilate it once more, that Achilles asks why his grievance cannot make dead the dead.

If Priam looks on Achilles as unbearably cruel in his desecration, then Achilles looks on Hector's body and sees not Hector, but the now-dead man who put Patroclus to death.

Achilles is the cause of Priam's grievance and the

source of his grief.

For Priam, the specter of Patroclus is but faint.

For Achilles, one imagines, at some unknown moment Hector and Patroclus constitute each other, mutually.

XII.

The constitutive force of this mutuality, one that is entirely of Achilles's making, forecloses nothing.

In its repetition, the day after day desecration of the dead that Achilles will not allow to be buried, the desecration that is the simultaneous remembering of the buried body, this mutuality triangulates.

In avenging his friend, in desecrating the enemy of his friend who put to death his friend, Achilles is himself remade.

The brutal act of self-making through desecration; through desecration, grievance, grief, and love.

The brutal act of self-making that is also self-undoing.

Achilles makes of himself a question for himself.

XIII.

What Achilles is undergoing is lost on Priam, who looks on from a distance, the distance of enemy lines.

Priam is of this drama, but he participates only as a minor figure.

Priam looks on, his helplessness reaffirmed every day. Every time Achilles acts against the dead body of his son, Priam is denied the right to bury Hector.

Priam is pathos. Achilles is a futile fury.

No wonder, then, that the intensity of the drama derives from that of its author, Achilles. It is the loyal friend and not the grief-stricken father, unable to fulfill his parental duty, who is Homer's central actor.

XIV.

And yet, while both Achilles and Priam are grief-stricken, it is only the father who knows how to grieve.

It is only the father who undertakes the work of confronting the loss of a loved one.

Priam opens himself to his grief, grapples with it, looks on Achilles's fury. And grieves all the more.

Priam's capacity for grief is endless.

Such a being toward death, toward the death of a loved one, appears antithetical to Achilles.

Achilles takes, as he must, the long road toward grief.

And even as he does, it seems a destination at which he is unlikely to arrive.

Is it only by doing the work of grieving that it becomes possible to know grief?

Must grief be thought of as that moment in time when we arrive at love?

When we know grief, no matter that it is an incomplete knowing, only then do we know love.

Like love, grief can open up, against all expectations, vistas unknown, horizons of being toward love previously unimaginable.

But grief never offers these prospects without cost.

Sometimes we can only come to know these prospects at the risk of a terrible violence.

A violence we execute against the other as much as against ourselves.

In learning to grieve for love, must we retain our capacity to grieve ourselves?

How can we know such a grief?

Is such a grieving possible without a symmetrical grievance against the self?

Or as an asymmetrical grievance against the self?

XV.

Through refraction, unobservable to Priam, grief and grievance, love and hate, combine in Achilles so that he comes to upstage the dead, the buried and the desecrated, through the sheer force of his helplessness.

It is the gods who deny Achilles his justice.

It is Achilles who does violence to Priam.

Priam is subject to Achilles's will.

Achilles is at the mercy of Zeus, the highest authority.

They operate in distinct registers, the one higher than the other, and so they are made to submit, each according to the appropriate scale.

Achilles belongs in the higher register because his grief deforms his grievance, his love complicates his hatred, his tendency toward isolation does not preclude fraternity.

Achilles acts as though he were master of his own fate and yet still knows, without acknowledging it, that he is but the plaything of the gods.

XVI.

The plaything of the gods.

A plaything of two conniving Spartan brothers.

But for all that, a figure who can make us turn again, against him, against what it is we think we know.

About grief and grievance.

Achilles: a restive figure.

Achilles, in grief and grievance, will not let us rest.

XVII.

Achilles.

A name to remember.

Achilles.

No one can forget his name.

We will meet him again.

Fragments I
Time, Names

It makes archiving an active interpretation, one is that selective, productive qua reproductive, productive of a "making-known" narrative as much as reproductive of images: know-how of making-known.

—Jacques Derrida,
The Beast and the Sovereign, Volume I

I.

Memory is the archive of grievance. Memory is the archive of grievance made visual, telekinetic, and narrativized. Through narrative, the story of having to endure historic loss, having been subjected to suffering, been witness to the failure of democratic process, all means must be employed. No offense is too small, no transgression must be overlooked. All pressures must be brought to bear to keep the time of grievance alive, alive and politically volatile. Grievance, as much as it is a struggle to restore time to itself (ahistory), sets itself against past and future and is apt to recover any and all times in which it first bloomed. The time of grievance is a single-minded project: the desire to reinstate the time that was permanently. For all the intensity of the commitment to ahistory, grievance is in a constant struggle to overcome its own lack of precision. Grievance is haunted by, as much as borne out of, that unanswerable question, When? When was the injury first inflicted? It is a question that cannot, no matter its articulative force, suffice. Instead, the very moment in which the transgressive act is committed, an act only rarely brought to life and an act that is almost never reckoned with, must be pronounced. Repeatedly. Kept alive via the image, constantly renewed through narrative.

Grievance does not need to inquire as to how one set of injuries, one experience of displacement or subjugation, concatenates with another. Grievance needs only to reassure itself that these injuries, displacements, injustices, and humiliations *are*: they have been endured, and now they must be redressed.

The transgressive act, for all its memorialization, is made immaterial and incidental by time. However, for all its lack of substance, it stands as the unimpugnable thing itself. In fact, it may be that its lack of substance is what gives the transgressive act—the fact of having been acted against—its Kantian ethos. *Ding an sich*: the thing-in-itself, if we permit ourselves a certain irony. The thing in its truth. Grievance as the time of the noumenon.

What we have nominated as ahistory. Grievance is that time determined by distinction. By its distinction from history. Grievance is premised on distinguishing itself resolutely from all other time because it is Edenic time. All other time belongs to the lapsarian. That time when the aggrieved was forced out of ahistory, against their will, into history. The lapsarian, for all its indistinction (what is the exact moment of the fall?), marks that moment when the aggrieved fall out of ahistory. And into grievance. The aggrieved is unceremoniously deposited in history by the other. Grievance is a relationship to time that is both determinate—the Edenic, ahistory—and constitutively indeterminate, which lends grievance an indeterminacy imbued with political fecundity. Political fecundity is the "know-how" of "making known."

Grievance, we can agree, is possessed of an ingeniousness in this art of "knowing how" to "make known."

Out of this fecundity, which also gives grievance what Adorno names a "vulgar idealism," grievance seeks to make time reach back to ahistory, always with the intention of extending that time into infinity. At the same time, eviscerated from the narrative of the aggrieved are all those threads that draw the authority and authenticity of the narrative into question, that threaten to undermine it and, in so doing, reduce or even negate its narrative and tele-kinetic force.

Out of this fecundity, grievance can continually replenish, update, review, revivify, edit/editorialize, transcribe, and publicize its own archive. The work of the archive of grievance is to keep the archive of grievance at once historic and current, an unblemished window onto the present-past, a kaleidoscopic rendering of the present-past; all documents—that is, events—are subject to being written out, relocated (to a place of greater or lesser significance), and refurbished. Adding gloss, the patina that is moral righteousness, to ahistory is second nature to grievance.

Every new generation of archivists makes available a different, more appropriate version of itself. With an enviable diligence, every new iteration constructs an archive more appropriate for the present-past moment of consumption. Is this the truth of "vulgar idealism"? That it subscribes, to an unscrupulous degree, to the logic of needs must? That it will present injury where others see only perjury? The perjuring of history in order that ahistory can be felicitous to itself? And that it will adopt infelicitous methods to achieve this outcome?

II.

In the United States, white grievance takes history as its target. White grievance cannot be about the future. It is always about either retrieving the past or holding the past in its temporal place. Thereby making of the present always the past-present. The present true to the political order that obtained in the past. The past-present mitigates against time—and the order that it upholds—being usurped by the present; or, worse, the order of the past-present being obliterated to history. Or, even worse, condemning the past-present to historical ignominy. To make of it, truly, a time not only past but also intolerable to the present, to say nothing of the past-present's unsustainability in the future. The past-present as odious to the future. The past-present as being over-taken by the event of the future; by the event that is the future.

White grievance as firmly opposed to the Hitchcockian fatalism of *The Man Who Knew Too Much* variety. White grievance will not abide the logic of inexorability exuded in *Que Sera, Sera*. It subscribes instead to the infallible truth that is: what was must always be. Then, now, and for all time.

White grievance refuses the teleological. Time must not be allowed to unfold, to take its own course. All danger to what was resides in releasing time from the grip of what must always be. Time must be made subservient. Time must be servant. Released into itself, time itself, understood as the harbinger of disorder, poses the single greatest threat to what must always be. Time must be held hostage lest it unleash all the threats contained within it. Time as the most dangerous enemy of what must always be.

What must always be as that force that puts an end to history. What must always be is about naming and maintaining a status quo—holding in place that moment in history when history punctuates itself. Permanently. To impose on history one unalterable time: the time of *what is*. All history as subject to the force that is what is.

The upending of what is makes of grievance a specific articulation. The desire of the aggrieved to right the wrongs committed by time. Once more we can rely, if not entirely, then still largely, on the unique force of the noun.

IIA. An Aphoristic Interlude

The unique force of the noun has become a phenomenon saturating all our communications, informing, cauterizing, and indeed mis-/shaping all our exchanges.[11] Instead of the noun signaling the start of a thought-filled, event-bearing predicate, the work of the noun is at once subverted and expanded. Subverted because it is relieved of primary function, provoking thought, and conscripted into the work of discursive extension. The noun as that grammatical part that is redolent in its self-sufficiency. The noun, especially the proper noun, as rhetorical, philosophical, and political stand-in for all that is supposedly contained within it, for all that is presumed to be attached to it. With the noun so construed as an all-purpose part of speech, it remains only then to utter the noun and a set of assumptions follow, as if axiomatically. Through the simple act of speaking the noun, the listener is supposed to have learned something, or is assumed to be—or, maybe, become—allied with something; dialectically, the simple utterance locates speaker and/or listener as opposed to something, that something that the noun projects. The noun, then, as not only self-sufficient but as constitutively self-exceeding. The noun as inveterately more and less than itself.

Two sets of names stringently opposed to each other. On the wrong side, so to speak, King George III's imperial rule. Abraham Lincoln. Abraham Lincoln freeing the slaves. Appomattox. Reconstruction. Educating the slaves.[12] The Negro franchise. *Brown v Board of Education*. Civil rights. Black Power. The 2020 presidential election.

On the side of the aggrieved stand the Declaration of Independence, Lee, Stonewall Jackson, Bedford Forrest, the grandfather clause, the literacy test, Jim Crow, *Plessey v Ferguson*, Bull

Connor, George Wallace, January 6.

For the aggrieved time must be made to take its place in the witness box of history as the accused. Accused of violence against the aggrieved, accused of having uprooted the aggrieved from its proper place in history, accused of contravening the historic agreement between the aggrieved and what-must-always-be. Can we name what-is and what-must-always-be *ahistory*? Not ahistorical, but a version of history that insists freezing itself at that moment in time most propitious for the aggrieved. Ahistory: where time is made to stand still. Forever. Ahistory is not antihistory. It is, rather, that mode of being in the world in which all modes of being are consolidated into the unchanging same, freezing time into that which had heretofore seemed impossible: the timelessness of time.

II. Continued

> The story of the glory
> Of the men who wore the gray
> In their graves, so still;
> The story of the living,
> Unforgiven yet forgiving,
> The victims still of hate
>
> —Father Ryan,
> "The men who wore the gray"[13]

Time is what makes violence against the aggrieved possible. In time is lodged the unspeakable loss suffered by the aggrieved. "The victims still," one presumes, "of [the] hate" Father Ryan so lamented in 1882 from his perch in Richmond, Virginia, the capital of the Confederacy. Only by inveighing and acting against time can things be set right—ahistory, the only account of human events that accords the aggrieved their proper place in time. For the aggrieved, time must be made subject to it, so much so that time will be made the exclusive property of the aggrieved. It is only in and through ahistory that the aggrieved will no longer be made to endure the "slings and arrows" of their outrageous "fortune."

What-was stands as the idealized time, that epoch in which time was wholly felicitous to the now-aggrieved subject of history. The aggrieved only comes into history, out of ahistory, in that moment when it is made to suffer time's untimely betrayal.

The acting of the aggrieved, violence, whether that be the Civil War, the Klan, Bull Connor's dogs, or the January 6 insurrection, always presents itself as the only possible—and legitimate—response to the injury done to the aggrieved. Ground out of a logic as dialectical as it is Newtonian in cast—every action has an equal and opposite reaction.

Grievance is the language produced out of aggrieved entitlement that politically miscasts itself as the injury done to ahistory. Following this logic, January 6 is (staged) injury as justifiable grievance.

In the economy of violence that is grievance, the aggrieved is always the only subject who has been victimized, wronged by history. As a historically powerful victim, it retains to itself the structural and political means to restore order to time. The aggrieved, as has already been intimated, has a rare gift for political irony. Like Malcolm X, it reserves to itself the right to restore order by "any means necessary."

IIB. Aphoristic Interlude

The aggrieved would find it inconceivable that Malcolm X could have cause for grievance.

No matter that, as Spike Lee's Malcolm X so lacerates the founding myth that is the Pilgrims' arrival on American soil, "We didn't land on Plymouth Rock. Plymouth Rock landed on us."

How could there be cause for grievance in so unfortunate an incident? Would the aggrieved not recommend that Malcolm X strike his best Sisyphean pose and get on with the work at hand? As a true Puritan undoubtedly would. And is the task that Malcolm X, malcontent that he is, must do not simpler than the one assigned Sisyphus? Instead of rolling the boulder up the hill, again and again until the end of time, all Malcolm X has to do is throw off the boulder.

As the American revolutionaries threw off British rule.

All that Malcolm X needed was to hand. He had only to call it into use.

But Malcolm X did not tarry with the myth of Sisyphus for one reason above all else.

Like Patrick Henry and Crispus Attucks, like Senator Wade (OH), Malcolm X dreamed of revolution, of overthrowing the status quo.

By any means necessary. Thereby serving notice of his grievance. Thereby alerting the descendants of the Pilgrims to a grave truth: their grievance was unequal to his.

The aggrieved would consider Malcolm X's claim to grievance a perjury. A violence against ahistory.

II: Continued

Revolutionary War, Civil War, state-adjacent violence (KKK), states' rights (Alabama, Mississippi, et al. during the civil rights struggle), a predominantly white insurrection encouraged by a defeated president. "Fight like hell." In order, no doubt, to ensure not so much the retelling of "The story of the glory" but rather for the January 2021, edition of this "story" an altogether more "glorious" ending. In other words, January 6 must tell "The story of the living." Of those who would restore the honor "Of those who wore the gray/in their graves so still." Of those who would triumph over "hate."

III.

To enjoin the aggrieved to "fight like hell" is to mobilize grievance through the production of what Jay Fliegelman, in his study of the writing of the Declaration of Independence, names "assent."[14] To issue that call in the twenty-first century is to tap into an eighteenth-century discourse that understands not only how to manufacture the language of grievance but also how to deliberately bring dissent into civil society. To enjoin is to give license to "fight like hell."

It is, moreover, to operate in the spirit of Benjamin Franklin's *Autobiography*, where Franklin counsels the art of presenting the transgressive—the illegal act that brings lawlessness into the public square—as eminently "reasonable." Franklin's rendering of "reasonable" arouses enormous suspicion, to say nothing of caution. After all, under the latitude he affords that term, all kinds of political mischief and ideological travesties can be committed. All under the rubric of "plain style," of what we may understand to be the clarity of speech, the obviousness of meaning, and, as January 6 leaves in no doubt, the immediacy of effect (Fliegelman 55).

What other interpretation could "fight like hell" possibly have? After all, the rhetorical strategy of the Declaration was to effect a "moving of passions," a set of "passions" that proved itself easily appropriable by the likes of Bedford Forrest, Bull Connor, and a defeated ex-president (43).

We are left, more than 200 years later, to come to terms with the residual effects of Franklin's cynical rendering. To deploy "reasonable" in so calculated a way is to know in advance that it will sanction, a priori, all actions undertaken by the aggrieved as a "legitimate response," borne of injustice. This gives a fortiori license to the aggrieved to present themselves, at critical junctures, as victims of a "corrupt" political system or as being targeted by a "two-tier" or "weaponized justice system." Franklin's "reasonable" echoes into, and thus haunts the political rhetoric of, our moment. It persists as a willfully erroneous misrepresentation: the deliberate mobilization of the discourse of reason, so key to figures such as Paine, Jefferson, and Franklin in that early Enlightenment moment, to accomplish nefarious ends.[15] If not in their day, then certainly in ours.

As a "rationalizing faculty," as well as an eighteenth-century nationalizing one, reason had the effect of reaching the "heart" of its target constituency.

Has the US populace reached the point where it is impervious to any reasoning that is not inherently

cynical? Or have we failed to detect the inherent cynicism all along, even in its most egregious
articulations?

What you sow, Benjamin Franklin, so shall you
reap. How are we to trace the path from Franklin
to the January 6 insurrectionists, except as a phantasm that never ceases to haunt? Sometimes there
is nothing to do but make your way through the
muck.

Blackbath

> The truth was obscure,
> Too profound and too pure,
> To live it you had to explode
>
> —Bob Dylan[16]

There is no need for us to delude or censor ourselves. The truth is axiomatic. The truth is by no means "obscure." It is certainly neither "profound" nor "pure." If an equivalent number of, or even fewer, far fewer, black bodies had gathered at the Capitol, crashed through protective barriers, assaulted police officers, and stormed the houses of Congress, very few would have lived to have their day in court. There would have been zero tolerance for such an attack on the "people's House." There would have been few, if any, arrests.

What black person would have dared to even mock defecate on the Speaker of the House's desk?

Is there any black person who would even imagine threatening to "hang" the vice president? And live to tell the tale?

Not even in our wildest dreams. In fact, at some unspeakable, visceral level, black America was chilled to the bone by the sight of a white lynch mob on the loose. A white lynch mob moving largely unimpeded. This is how the history of lynching repeats itself: the first time as a tragedy unforgettable to the black psyche; the second time as the specter of white-on-white violence, a violence that did not culminate in white death. The threat of violence where everyone lived to tell the tale.

As Toni Morrison might have it, "And the difference is all the difference there is." The difference between life and death. The difference between black death and white life.

And so it is that black people in America would have been sure of only one outcome on that day of white grievance run amok. Black America would have been able to proclaim, without hesitation, "We are all Ashli Babbitt." That would have been the fate of a black American insurrection. There would have been no need for it to be written. It would have been preordained.

There would have been no mainstream self-congratulation every time an insurrectionist was sentenced to a five- or twelve-year jail term. Or worse, was labeled a "peaceful tourist."

"Due process" is due only the aggrieved.

Who doubts that there would have been a bloodbath, one justified by a liberal state and all its many repressive apparatuses? Or should we say a *blackbath*?

To act on a grievance is a right afforded only to white America. A right hard won with the blood of those who lie resting "in their graves so still." Father Ryan's magnanimous Confederates, "Unforgiven, yet forgiving."

For the other there is only the guarantee of the "butcher's bill."[17]

The other will always be made to pay for any transgression the aggrieved commit in the name of grievance.

The "butcher's bill" is always bloodstained. Soaked with the blood of the other. We know who pays.

The promise is eternal: the South will rise again. A consolidated South this time, not circumscribed by geography but comprising a South of the aggrieved imaginary. That is, a South that drew into its ambit North, Midwest, Southwest, West, and, yes, of course, the physical South. Not so much the Confederacy as the confederation of the like-minded. The like-minded aggrieved. A constituency with the capacity for infinite growth.

In the contemporary North, in the Midwest, in the Southwest and the West, the Southern state of mind is but a stone's throw away. At most, a county or two removed.

A constituency that enthusiastically embraces Patrick Henry's revolutionary fervor, an injunction delivered to the House of Burgesses in 1765: "If this be treason, make the most of it."[18] Out of that radical spirit, the Virginian would craft his most famous pronouncement a decade later: "Give me liberty, or give me death!" The eighteenth-century revolutionary life would be lived in terms Dylanesque: "To live it you had to explode."

Grievance is the tie that binds. For all the differences in ideology, their different visions of and for the Republic, and political motivation, grievance is the tie that binds Henry to Father Ryan to Bull Connor to the January 6 insurrectionists. Making further allowance, of course, for that which distinguishes the potential revolutionary martyr, Henry (who is prepared to die), from the insurrectionists, who wish only to inflict death on the other. Even an other, the white vice president, who does not conform to the profile of the other.

The Confederated South is where Father Ryan's "hate" is resurrected. Out of the ashes of the undefeatable, the South will once more rise. This time, it hopes, out of the universality of white grievance.

Grievance is more American than apple pie. Grievance is the indestructible metaphysics of the aggrieved. A metaphysics that, all evidence to the contrary, continues to insist upon itself as "profound" and "pure."

IV.

So brazen and self-assured is the aggrieved in its grievance, a confidence imbued, ironically, by history, that it is rarely deterred from its historically violent ways. The injustice inflicted by history legitimates all aggrieved actions. Grievance as more than simply immunizing the aggrieved against the law. The law is made to accord with the actions of the aggrieved so that the actions constitute, post ipso facto, the law. In a signal inversion of legal history, the law itself becomes the consequence of a precedent. Under the law that is white grievance, *stare decisis* is not the prior legal decision but rather the precedent established by the actions of the aggrieved.

January 6: the mass mobilization of the aggrieved. A tumultuous gathering convened, knowingly or not, in the cause of grievance. Which always means to redress grievance. To set right a wrong.

The aggrieved secures for itself, and for itself only, the right to punish. To punish, as it sees fit, those whom it deems worthy of punishment by virtue of having acted against the ahistoric rights of the aggrieved. The relationship between grievance and rights was crucial to the conception and writing of the Declaration. In fact, "The Declaration concludes with a mutual pledge to support the step of independence; but that is preceded by a preamble stating the rights at issue, and a list of grievances infringing those rights."[19]

In the name of grievance, the aggrieved understands itself to be acting against all who "infringe" upon their "rights." And out of and in the name of a chiasmatic love. In the name of "love," insurrection is patinaed, inflected, crossed with the logic of *causa damnata est iusta causa*. The "pledge" that bound the thirteen colonies is revealed now as more binding than that *conquistador* sui generis Jefferson could ever have imagined. The value of the "pledge" is that it can always be activated. Again. American grievance can always attach itself to a right. A right infringed upon must, perforce, find its proper articulation as a grievance.

A veritable article of white American faith. In grievance we trust.

Without ever forgetting the force attached to both white right and grievance. That force which ensures that might makes right.

Etat voyous.

Jefferson considered America a nation conquered by King George's subjects.

John Adams, keen student of the British charter, did not share Jefferson's outlook.

Grievance thus contrives itself as a love that goes by the name of "democracy" or "free and fair elections," both of which set themselves against injustice; injustice that goes by the name of, say, "stolen elections," "election fraud," or "election interference." In the case of January 6, these names achieved proprietary status, such as Dominion Voting Systems.

In the name resides an ambition riddled with irony. Grievance seeks to establish its "dominion" over time, over space, and over every electoral outcome that does not subscribe to the logic of grievance. That it cannot establish such "dominion" is what grievance chafes against.

Aphorisms IV
Thinking, Grief.
Thinking Grief

I.

Is that moment when we will not even undertake to think for grief the moment when grief becomes grievance?

When grief metastasizes into grievance?

Do we ever think the proximity of grief to grievance? Dare we look into the abyss of indistinction at just that moment before grievance overwhelms grief?

II.

Would we not be best served by summoning up our courage to look into this very abyss of indistinction, at that very moment when indistinction is about to give way to difference?

III.

If this is how grief gives us to think, can we not say that grief is the most instructive, the most redolently philosophical, of all affects? Is it not, before all else, out of grief that we should think? Think grief? Is it not grief that we should hold dear because it may be all that can inoculate us against the virulence of grievance?

IV.

Is grievance a virus for which there is no antidote?

V.

If grievance is so virulent a force, should we not pause a moment and contemplate our grief, so that we may be able to take its full measure? That we may learn to treasure grief?

VI.

How can we let ourselves be in our grief? Can we open ourselves up to our grief? Can we take the time to learn to know the time of grief?

VII.

Should we not ask what we lose when we grieve no more? Do we not already intuit what we lose when we grieve no more?

VIII.

Is our world not most ripe for thinking when we give ourselves to grief? What possibilities for thinking our being does grief present to us?

IX.

Is grief the time most fit—most fitted—for thinking? If the time of grief is so fitted, why have we for so long not availed ourselves of what grief presents? What grief makes present to us?

X.

Is it only in the time of grief that we think both *Sein und Zeit*? Is this not already our strongest intuition?

Aphorisms V
Grief, Grievance:
In Music, in Literature

I.

Is it only through grief that we come to glimpse human fellow feeling? That we show ourselves, even under the bloodiest circumstances, capable of something other than we think ourselves capable of? Is grief so overwhelming that we have not, even as it colors our visage and we look it directly in the face, within ourselves the capacity to name it? Is grief so overwhelming as to make it recognizable to us in moments of unspeakable loss, in the moment that follows an unspeakable, unjustifiable violence? Does grief exceed, by some considerable measure, loss? How would we think for that which lies on the far side of loss?

Does persecution lie on the far side of loss, or does it

cut closer to the bone?

Can persecution only be borne by the joke?

II.

Is the memory of persecution always in the joke?

Hiding in plain sight?

Charles Barkley, in an Alabama voice wrapped in an Auburn smile: "I am not going back to being black and poor."

The joke intensifies.

Barkley is only half right.

As a rich man he is unlikely to go back to being poor.

As a black man, he never stopped being black.

At least Barkley has that to fall back on.

Half a grievance.

III.

If the persecuted derives from a line of double execution, must the joke be twice as funny for the other to live with a joke that can only be told at its own expense?

Is the joke a form of expiation, a belated attempt to control history, or does it increase the burden borne by the other?

It is said that if you're laughing, the whole world

laughs with you. Surely, however, if the joke you are telling is on you, there lurks always the suspicion that the joke will cost you. For the persecuted it is better not to be the butt of the joke.

What kind of expert does that make the other? Is it an expertise anyone really wants to acquire?

Is it always better to tell the joke about your own persecution than be made into an object of ridicule or scorn if *your* joke is expropriated? Turned against you? Surely this makes the joke a form of ownership too, over which a struggle is always likely to ensue.

Does the other telling the joke against itself constitute a form of self-possession? Joke possession?

IV.

Is the joke the last best prophylactic against history?

Langston Hughes was of a such a mind.

We laugh to keep from crying, he said of the Negro.

Even as Bessie Smith wailed.

Even as Lady Day could barely contain her pain, in a music most tragically beautiful.

Is the joke always the most haunted form of self-expression?

Can the joke stand against music?

Or, in Robbie Robertson's case, can the music stand against the truth of the joke?

Or is it only in music that the joke finds its truth?

James Baldwin found his truest truth in Bessie Smith.

V.

Are we capable of such a thinking that takes unto itself persecution, poetry, pain, and hope that promise salvation through the blues, and only through the blues? And if not, is that not the horizon upon which we should set our thinking?

How is it that we have not yet set our thinking upon such a horizon?

How will we ever teach the self to distinguish between grief and grievance if we do not work toward the making of such a horizon?

Grievance affords the aggrieved the right to wallow in grievance.

Grievance is a form of self-indulgence in which there is always the capacity for violence—against the other.

Grievance is self-righteous to a fault, so it turns the aggrieved firmly from thinking.

Grievance is the force of contraction. It hardens the world. Makes of it a smaller place, a place in which the aggrieved are relieved of the work of thinking the self in the world.

Grievance knows only what it knows.

It knows, refuses to know, anything beyond what it knows.

Grief has been pained into knowing that it does not know what it is now learning, slowly, painfully.

Grief opens itself to what it does not know.

By the same token, grief knows that much that must be known remains unknowable to the grieving.

VI.

Self-righteousness is the empty performance of pieties that cannot obscure the failure to do what is right and proper.

A little like those who, in announcing themselves to be acting in accordance with what they proclaim to be right, declare themselves to be "acting on their principles."

This is the language of the charlatan.

This pronouncement can only issue from the mouth of untruth.

This is the speech of the dissembler.

This is the utterance of those who would give the veneer of political respectability to their disreputable motives.

We should give a wide berth to those who insist that they are acting on their principles.

It remains only for us to discern their ulterior motive.

They mobilize for mischief, those who act on their principles.

We should treat them as Polonius directs in advice to his son, Laertes: "To thine own self be true."

It is the voice of self-interest. Wrapped in self-righteousness.

It is a voice soon to be stilled by death. A proper fate for Polonius. And perhaps a fate that should be a cautionary tale for all those who bloviate and pretend otherwise.

Or, more tragically, bloviate but do not know otherwise.

Or, comically, those who bloviate because they have no other mode of address.

Borrow not from such a man, lend not to such a woman.

Mistake them not for friends.

One would do better to keep company with Judas Iscariot. There is more loyalty to be found in a disciple who knows his price.

And whatever you do, seek not their counsel.

For they are always their own principal.

VII.
Grief is the most excruciating mode of learning to know.

Grief is an encounter with a rare form of self-instruction.

Grief is an unforgiving taskmaster. Sometimes brutal.

Always exacting. Extracting a price.

1765.

The British Parliament.

The Stamp Act.

The imposition of a financial duty.

Exacting from the colonies for legal, commercial documents; exacting for the spreading of news.

1776.

A revolution.

Not a revolution for "Stamp Paid."

Such a name Toni Morrison gives us in *Beloved*. A name fit for grief.

A name that can exact nothing.

A name that can enact nothing.

"Stamp Paid." The name of an unpaid act.

"Stamp Paid." The name of an unpayable act.

The name for which there can be no recompense.

The name for which there can be no payment forward.

Or back toward the past.

Not in the time of revolution.

Not in the Ohio of the Civil War.

Not in any time.

His proper name is patinaed with love.

It is, unquestionably, Stamp Unpayable.

Is *Beloved* the recognition that there can be no depositing against an unpayable debt?

The debt can never be diminished.

It grows.

Jes Grew.

That is why the boatman is given a name that is made only to give.

The boatman takes his name from a distant land.

In time removed but never distant.

The boatman lives close to 1765.

1765 is no more removed from him than 1862.

"Stamp Paid" is a time endlessly exacting.

Of ceaseless extraction.

No creditor would approach Queequeg.

Of "Stamp Paid," however, they have no fear.

The tides of time, driven by the determination to capture those who sought freedom, always threaten to wash the boatman away.

His is a name as much for grief as for a boatman who watches for the runaway and tries to keep grief at bay just a moment longer.

A name for a boatman who knows that there is grief in life. It is so.

Grief insists that the self undertake to teach itself what it does not know.

Grief instructs the self into what it must teach itself to know.

Grief makes no promises that the self will learn that which it needs to know.

Grief forecloses nothing.

Grief shuts off no avenue of learning.

Grief prefers profligacy to economy. Sometimes.

Grief looks kindly on those who know their limits and then proceed to exceed them.

Grief cannot abide those who do not give their grief its due.

Grief alone knows that there is love in suffering.

"Suffer little children to come unto me."

Grief submits itself to lore.

Grief will not make itself subservient to the law. Antigone will bury Polynices, regardless of the punishment that Creon visits upon her.

Grieving is Hippocratic: grieving, learn to heal thyself.

Grief hews closely to philosophy's foundation: *gnothi seauton*.

Grief, know thyself. As grief.

Grief reminds the grieving that there will be no end to what must be learned.

What a task grief sets the grieving.

VIII.

Achilles. Twice denied love.

Once by death, the other by injustice. And military incoherence.

Menelaus goes to war because his wife, Helen, has been seduced away.

War, Trojan, ensues.

Menelaus is intent on extracting recompense.

Not from the enemy; that will have to wait. But from an ally.

Cuckolded, Menelaus claims Briseis, lover of Achilles.

Grievance has many points of origin.

The more localized the point, the greater the intensity.

The greater the effects.

The higher the personal cost, the more expansive the political fallout.

Agamemnon, commanding general, proves himself a loyal sibling, and not a just commander.

Out of heartbreak, there is nothing left for Achilles, wrongly deprived of love, but a brooding anger. And retreat.

Love breeds an inarticulable grief.

Love wrongly denied gives birth to justifiable grievance.

In Achilles, grief and grievance lose their distinction.

Like in George Floyd.

One festers in the other, nurtured by the other.
Is grievance that which we face when grief turns an angry shade of septic?

In Achilles, grief and grievance merge into a raging torrent of heartache.

A love triangle.

Achilles.

Patroclus.

Briseis.

The triangulation of love and loss, grief and grievance.

Grief churns in grievance, grievance finds a turbulent sustenance in grief.

In Achilles we can no longer know grievance from grief.

In Achilles the difference is eviscerated, leaving us confounded.

As if we know nothing of grief.

As if grievance were a stranger to us.

As if grievance, left to itself, is a thing to marvel at.

As if our grievance reveals the mendacity of our time.

As if we have polluted the beauty of grievance, the tragic, soaring beauty of grievance.

All because we do not want to know what losing love can do.

We are the benighted offspring of Menelaus.

We know Achilles too much only because we think him too little.

We know Achilles not at all.

David Malouf, sensing our depravity and wishing to

guard against our worst inclinings, gives him another name. *Ransom*.

A name that betrays too much.

A name conceived in rectitude.

That leaves us naked in our base proclivities.

As if our crime against grievance is that we have lost all appetite for the epic.

As if we were right, all along, to be afraid of that fatal conjunction: grief and grievance.

Achilles gives us everything to think again.

What know we of grief and grievance?

Is it only Achilles who can make us turn from where we are?

Turn away so that we are made, once more, to face Greece.

Made wary of Sparta's militarism.

No longer willing to trust the fate of grief and grievance to the sons of Atreus.

Athens still remains. For Jacques Derrida.

Athens remains, as must have first been sighted from a promontory in Algiers.

Following Derrida, the figure of Derek Walcott, looming, large, casting the Caribbean Sea into shadow.

The flotsam and jetsam of history washing up on sunbathed shores.

Omeros.

The sparkling sea.

Thanatos.

The opacity of death.

Leaving us, uncertain contemporaries, uncertain in our contemporaneity with Homer, Derrida, Walcott, Jean Rhys.

We wait, unsure of how to take our place in line.

Why will we not wail for Achilles?

Do we not wail because we dare not think our own grief?

Do we hope that we too, like Agamemnon, can stand aside when the tide of grief crashes onto the shores of grievance?

Is there no poesis to our grief?

No splendid name for our grievance?

Are we worthy of nothing but the King of Grievance?

Is the shaman the shameful house in which our pathos takes refuge?

Would we not prefer a hut, unsteady in construction, threatened by the strength of the incoming tide, but in which we can evince an outlook sturdy enough to face the uncertainties that come from the sea?

IX.

Can we only be redeemed by the singular grief-grievance of Achilles?

It is a good thing that Achilles refuses to abandon us.

Achilles, a man of deep thought, does not trust us to our own devices.

Is it only Achilles who can save us from the putrid grievance of our loathsome selves?

Achilles makes us live in hope of grief.

X.

There is a harshness particular to grief. A harshness encountered nowhere else.

Grief can assume the appearance of the unfeeling.

It is, however, a harshness that keeps grief distinct from grievance.

Grievance is the first but by no means only victim of its own certitude.

The other often comes to grief because of the certitude of the aggrieved.

Grievance extracts. Grief extracts, but it always holds out the prospect of replenishment.

Each exacts its own costs.

But only one offers the possibility of being in the world in a way different from how the self conducted itself before the event of loss.

Grief is the right to love that is a privilege only the living can enjoy. Grief reminds us of this.

To know persecution is to walk the path of loss.

To walk the path of loss is to commit, willingly or not, to venture into the unknown.

Grief is given to the living so that they might know what it is to live in preparation for dying.

Grief cannot be sustained without courage and fortitude and unbearable solitude.

In such a being, in one who loves, in one who looks upon persecution and is shaken but not broken by persecution, thinking finds a place to know grief.

XI.

Grief is gloriously constitutive of American literature.

From Herman Melville to W. E. B. Du Bois to Eugene O'Neill, from William Faulkner to Ralph Ellison to Lorraine Hansberry, from John Cheever to August Wilson to Don DeLillo, from Leslie Marmon Silko and Cormac McCarthy, grief abounds. The grief of the South Sea islander Queequeg, whose coffin is inscribed in a writing that, in its indigeneity, will forever remain illegible to Ishmael; grief for the loss of the firstborn that so haunts Du Bois; grief consumptive in O'Neill, intensely local and incestuous in Faulkner, tragic in Ellison and Hansberry, empty in Cheever, historical in Wilson, subdued and thoughtful in DeLillo, structural in Marmon Silko, and always bloody and violent in McCarthy.

At its apogee in Toni Morrison's *Beloved*.

Among the most famous addresses in American literature, 124 Bluestone Road, haunted. By grief. By death. By the return of the dead, murdered daughter, who, it would seem, demands to be loved—*beloved*—because she was never properly grieved. Resurrected so that she could be grieved. So she could be present while she was being grieved. Grieved in (the after-) life as she was not in death.

Grief unleashes deadly forces. Stamp Paid saves Sethe, who has murdered Beloved.

Beloved will not be forgotten.

In grief there is the love of remembering.

Grief loves to remember.

Grief reminds us to love.

Grief remembers love.

Grief reanimates love.

Grief is love.

For the living, if not for the dead, who can now watch the living as they grieve. And not only for her. Sometimes they grieve for themselves, without properly knowing it.

How does the mother who murdered her daughter so that her daughter would not have to live enslaved grieve for the dead-living daughter?

How does the sister who survived in utero make the sister who was put to death love her? Can the dead love the living?

Can only the mother who murdered the daughter know how to love that daughter?

Is it too fanciful to propose that only love can conquer grief?

Is grief a second chance at love? Is love only ever truly learned through grief?

The tears of grief conjoin to form the rivulets in which love can freely flow.

"Dearly Beloved, I have always loved you. In life as in death. I murdered you because I loved you. My love for you could only be made manifest as my grief. My grief is the surest evidence of my love. Forgive me. I love you. In life as in death."

"Dearly beloved, we are gathered here today in the name of love. To love."

What is not inscribed remains only to be inscribed.

Should every headstone be scrubbed clean and marked again, anew, this time? So that what was forgotten can now be written? So that what is inscribed can be more felicitous to the dead?

So that the love that was not written can be chiseled on, in a script now entirely sure of itself?

Is "Dearly Beloved" not a superfluity?

Is it only the living who wish to remind themselves that the dead are dearly beloved?

How can the living know that the dead are at peace in their love?

Beloved came back to be loved.

XII.

Can the living speak the truth of the dead?

What does grief render unspeakable?

Does grief delude, mislead, the living?

Does grief make the living forget even as they remember?

Are we not, before all else, to distrust our grief?

Are we too distraught to write properly of the dead in our grief?

A moratorium should be declared that prohibits inscription until grief knows its truth, however long it takes.

So that every inscription writes the love of grief in its proper time.

Beloved was twice a victim.

First she was the victim of a slave mother's love; then she fell victim to the limited sexual favors her slave mother had to trade.

To trade in exchange for inscription upon the headstone of the dearly departed.

The slave mother had enough only for "Beloved."

A name of no distinction. The name inscribed only in death.

A name made indistinct by its incompletion.

Not "Dearly Beloved." "Beloved."

Beloved brought grief, but does she not properly belong in the ranks of the aggrieved?

For she was wronged, surely, not once but twice.

Beloved's grievance is a terrible thing.

It can upturn furniture. It can almost make a house shake to its foundations.

It can make two brothers flee their home.

It can test the limits of love.

Only a mother can live with such a terrible love. And a sister, who wants to know of death.

It can drive out fraternal association.

It can make of a house a place of death.

It can lure the enslaved man from the past, but it cannot make of itself a hospitable abode.

Grief, grievance, love, slavery.

How is a house divided from slavery only by a river not to be haunted?

Grief and grievance can make the crossing from slave to free at will.

Anytime they wish.

Beloved is born a second time. A flood of water streams out from Sethe when Beloved is born again, at the moment of her own choosing.

Aggrieved that she could not die at her appointed time, Beloved came back to live again until she had exhausted her time.

XIII.

Grief is Queequeg in his call to Ishmael: "Call me love."

Grief is the call of love.

A queer love.

Grief is a queer love that sublates the unintelligibility of Queequeg's language.

But grief too has limits.

It insists: call me anything, but do not call me Ahab.

That is grievance.

Imperial, imperious grievance.

Driven-mad-by-grievance grievance.

Whale-sized grievance.

XIV.

Grief must be looked on with courage.

Like the student teacher Du Bois witnesses one summer among the tenant farmers who are barely scraping by in the "hills of Tennessee."

And fortitude. As Alexander Crummell does, neglected by his parishioners, rudely treated by the white authorities of the church he seeks to serve.

Grief gives to itself, without fail, a face. A face recognizable. A face made recognizable.

A memory imprinted in the face.

A face made in the image of the grieving.

The face of love turns away from grievance.

Grievance is composed of an undifferentiated multitude.

The exception in the undifferentiated multitude is exceptional only in tautological terms.

It is the exception that proves the rule of undifferentiation.

The shaman. Ashli Babbitt.

The exception is feigned nativity.

Lacking gravitas. Not a figure of Kurtzian proportions who could emerge out of the literary ferment and fecundity that was Joseph Conrad's anticolonial imagination.

Desirous of making itself the spectacle. That spectacle that has no vision of history.

Set always against solitude.

Not knowing that it is only the aptitude for solitude that gives the Magistrate of *Waiting for the Barbarians* foresight. The prescience to know that the empire cannot stand.

Colonel Joll, in his opacity, is the instrument of grievance. An instrument created by the colonial administration's bureaucracy and military might.

It will count for nothing. The empire will meet its end.

Colonel Joll's glasses are meant to make him inscrutable.

They serve only to blind him to what lies before him.

Colonel Joll mistakes the fisher people for the barbarians.

Colonel Joll cannot tell friend from enemy.

It is Colonel Joll who condemns the empire to its death, the victim of an indiscriminate grievance.

There is no distinguishing, for the empire, one other from another other.

The empire treats all others alike.

Its grievance against the other is universal.

Opacity obscures vision. Opacity will not see what is there to be seen.

XV.

The Magistrate can see the girl. He can tend to her. He learns to live with her. Maybe even to love her.

He will lose his friends for her.

The Magistrate will risk his life, and his livelihood, to give back to her the life, in a body now disfigured by imperial violence, that was once hers.

The Magistrate will grieve when the girl returns to her people.

The imperial outpost is left to face a ruin of its own making.

Grievance is ruinous. In its determination to exterminate the other, it is prone to destroying itself.

Gabriel García Márquez, wistful, cautions, *No One Writes to the Colonel*.

With his opaque eyewear, can Colonel Joll read?

Ruinous, yes, but grievance is not without menace. Never without menace.

In her death, Ashli Babbitt remains a menace.

A menace that in death could bring death to the other.

A menace to society.

But not on the order of *Menace II Society*.

Menace II Society speaks in the name of those menaced by society.

XVI.

In death, as in life, Ashli Babbitt remains a threat. She retains the capacity to menace those who have long been menaced by society.

Like the shaman, Ashli Babbitt emerges out of that place where the desire of the aggrieved for vengeance finds fertile soil. Ashli Babbitt is that *dispositif* of grievance that marks the reinforcement of the desire for retribution by a perjured ipseity.

Ashli Babbitt is what happens when the God-given right of the aggrieved to eternal power is thwarted.

And when this right is denied, grievance institutes, on the spot if necessary, its own system of justice.

Making the shaman and Ashli Babbitt the Northern grandchildren of Bull Connor.

The shaman is a showman, but Ashli Babbitt is the insurrectionist made martyr.

In martyring Babbitt, grievance shows itself to be a shameless form of sophistry.

XVII.

Grievance is, in Immanuel Kant's sense, heteronomous. It is loyal to its own desires, which override any sense of moral duty or reason.

Except, of course, that grievance, in its perjured ipseity, understands itself to be an exemplary moral creature governed by reason.

XVIII.

Grievance is fluent in only one language, revenge, but it is possessed of many idioms.

In each of these idioms lurks terror.

Sometimes the terror is of the generic variety. But most often it is recognizable only to that point where it seeks to distinguish itself.

Every iteration of grievance is intent on establishing its singularity.

As much as grievance requires a basic level of instruction, as soon as it finds its feet, it shows itself to be— like all other grievances—autogenerative.

Each will produce its own mechanisms. Each will establish its own procedures, bring into being its own system for adjudication. It will decide its method of indicting, prosecuting, sentencing.

In every sentencing, lenience is a stranger.

There are no mitigating factors.

Grievance is, a priori, just.

Those who act against the aggrieved must expect to be punished to the fullest extent of the law.

And the law, as we know, is mad.

Who would be mad enough to show lenience to the transgressor?

Again and again, parading the transgressor before its adherents, grievance proclaims, "Ecce homo."

This indictment comes to us from Judas Iscariot, but that fallen disciple as, in comparison with the aggrieved, a rank amateur when it comes to humiliating and persecuting the transgressor.

XIX.

Expedient too, showing itself adept at harnessing the dead to exact retribution from the other.

Grievance is soteriological.

It promises the aggrieved that salvation can be achieved.

It does not preach death, but neither does it shy away from the prospect of death, a fate that is rewarded with martyrdom.

Grievance knows how to make of the dead a cause for violence.

Self-righteous violence.

For the aggrieved, its own dead can be made instrumental in the instigation or prolongation of violence.

Let no death go unexploited.

For the dead of the aggrieved, a *cause célèbre* easily takes the place of mourning.

Grievance is its own best sustenance. To this end, a pretend martyr will do.

Grievance will raise its victims to that status which suits its purpose.

Grievance is as loud and spectacular as it is unscrupulous.

Grievance is strategic. It positions itself on the precipice of that which it assures itself will be the cause of a further grievance.

Grievance is maleficently creative. Endlessly generating grievances, new and old.

And yet, the aggrieved insist that it is only they who can protect against barbarism, against the impending apocalypse.

The aggrieved stand with Colonel Joll.

They are the last protectors of civilization.

The aggrieved will tarry no longer. Always ready to lunge into action.

The aggrieved will, in their being so aggrieved, take no advice from Martin Heidegger: "it could be now that prevailing man has for centuries now acted too much and thought too little."[20]

The aggrieved have waited long enough for the barbarians.

Time to hunt down the barbarians. Re-establish civilization.

They prefer the Colonel of *Waiting for the Barbarians* to his literary ancestor, *Heart of Darkness*'s Colonel.

Is what the aggrieved fear not the choice that literature provides them but a more horrific truth? That they would rather eschew such a choice? That they would give themselves over to both Joll and Kurtz? That for them the only proper choice is no choice?

"The horror, the horror." Twice over.

XX.

Grief knows that it will find no place to dwell in a being who will not deface Joll, rip off his opaque eyewear and make him see the empire as the Magistrate does.

The aggrieved look, but they cannot see. And even if they could, they would see only that which suits them.

To the aggrieved, the myopic appear as omniscient.

Grief knows that the horror lies in Kurtz. It does not derive from his surroundings. Kurtz sought such conditions as he needed. In finding them, his appetite for horror found a place where it could be satisfied. Being satisfied, it learned to thrive.

The Congo is like the Thames.

It is but a river.

Except that the river that is farthest from Marlow is the one that is closer to the Conradian heart of truth than the other river, the one more agreeable to Marlow.

One river makes the man come to see himself as he is. Allows him to embrace himself in all his frightening truth.

The other river is what allows for dissembling. From the banks of the other river emanates nothing but disingenuous narration. The other river keeps man himself at a remove from himself.

The other river, closest to the Intended, gives solace. It spares the Intended the truth of rejection. It spares the Intended truth. It is a costly business, this speaking from the other river.

Like knowing how to grieve, it requires courage to make the self look, without blinking, into the heart of darkness.

It is not a thing to be taken lightly, Édouard Glissant warns us, looking into the abyss.

"Peoples who have been to the abyss do not brag of being chosen … They live Relation and clear the way for it, to the extent that the oblivion of the abyss comes to them and consequently, their memory intensifies."

Is it only possible to look into the abyss after you have looked into the darkness of your own heart?

Would we rather not confront our Kurtz within? Kurtz startles us not because he is inconceivable. Kurtz frightens because he is all too recognizable.

"There but for the grace of God go I."

What intensity of memory resides in the heart?

What if we are not able to look into the heart of our own darkness?

Will we be ashamed at our lack of courage?

There is no need to brag about having been to the abyss because having been to the abyss is enough.

It needs no elaboration.

Especially if you are fainthearted.

XXI.

But who, we should ask, is really the fainthearted? The Intended, who does not know? Or Marlow, who writes overlooking the tranquility of the Thames?

Marlow, who promises the Intended that Kurtz's last word was the name of the Intended, is the first to turn from the horror.

What does Marlow fear is in his own heart?

Is the Intended not to be terrified at being the last name spoken? How could the Intended find succor in that? Is the last name spoken not the name of death?

"Dearly beloved, we are gathered here..." We are gathered in the name of death.

No death is without horror.

No one is without horror.

XXII.

Grief allows for the grieving of the horror such as is ours.

Grievance does not grieve.

Grievance does not want to learn to know grief.

Grievance cannot bear grief. Nor can it countenance the loss found at the heart of grief.

Grievance would be overwhelmed by grief.

Only grief can bear grief.

Grief is a mode of being saturated in bereavement.

Grief knows itself as that mode of being that follows being made bereft, of someone held dear, of something of immense value.

XXIII.

To be bereft is to be transformed.

It is to undertake the work of *after*. An after imposed on by the self, an after that is the consequence of contingency.

An after saturated in *before*.

It is to know that everything that belonged to the before has now been taken away.

It is to learn how to live with the specter of before.

It is to live in expectation of future encounters with the before.

It is to know that the before is no more, even as it persists. It is to know that the before shows no sign of abating.

It is to know the before in forms both eminently recognizable and utterly disfigured.

It is to inveigh against the violence inaugurated by the moment that is after.

It is to come to know inveighing against as futile.

And yet necessary. Unavoidable.

XXIV.

Only grief can bear the love that is grief.

To grieve is to think love.

To grieve is to learn to love to think.

To grieve is to give thanks to the other. In the name of the other. Out of love for the other.

Grief makes us turn to face the other, so that we might know our love for the other.

So that we may learn the language of the other.

So that we make our own language strange to ourselves.

In grieving, we come to know the strange joys of being alienated from ourselves.

Dearly beloved, we are gathered in the name of love.

XXV.

How it is that in grief we are given over to thinking?

There can be no grieving without thinking.

Denke est danke, says Heidegger. We nod in agreement. But we insist that it is necessary to add that grieving is thinking too. *Trauern is auch Denken*.

XXVI.

Would that thinking, rather than grievance, were more American than apple pie.

Would that we would give ourselves to grief, rather than submitting so easily to the siren's call that is grievance.

XXVII.

Would that it was us made the object of Judas Iscariot's scorn: "Behold the man."

XXVIII.

In looking on the face of this man, Judas must be shocked to see the profound helplessness of his grievance in the face of the grief this man feels for him.

What choice is left to Judas but to take his own life?

"Ecce homo," on the other hand, will take the torturous path—a common hanging given its own name, crucifixion—but he promises, this man, something beyond.

It is that "Ecce homo" offers what is unknown that makes him, and him alone, worth beholding.

XXIX.

In grievance lurks not only the capacity to instill terror in the other.

Grievance knows that it is itself encased in death.

An encasing of its own making.

Grievance cannot escape the fate to which it condemned itself.

But, then again, who is to say that Judas's grievance is not a singular one, in which death secured at the hand of the self is welcomed.

Fragments II
The State

Civil society is the true source and theatre of all history, and how absurd is the conception of history held hitherto, which neglects the real relationship and confines itself to high-sounding dramas of princes and states.

—Karl Marx, *The German Ideology*

I.

January 6 as the capacity of uncivil society to act within civil society as if it were the last line of defense against the very uncivility it is enacting. As if to lend credence to Marx's claim that "civil society is the true source and theatre of all history." In the logic of grievance, it is only the uncivil, in their militant upholding of civil society, who can guarantee its future. Civil society must be upheld and protected against the present—ahistory must prevail over history—and ahistory can only be assured by an act of violent uncivility. The logic of grievance is, of course, paradoxical because it proceeds from the assumption that only the aggrieved can procure civil society through uncivil violence. In this way, grievance presents the cure for uncivility as indistinguishable from the disease.

The sharpest contradiction is that the cure is the disease. Violence is the only cure for the disease even as violence constitutes the very incarnation of what would be presumed the greatest threat to civil society. The pathogen is itself the prophylaxis. Only that force which threatens can protect that which it threatens. Only the logic of grievance can sustain such a paradox: civil society can only be sustained through the enactment of violent uncivility.

The intensity of the paradox is such that one cannot be sure if it is a perverse form of autoimmunity or if the logic of grievance represents an extreme and radical form of autoimmunity.

What cannot be dismissed, however, is what Marx identifies as a "real relation." That is, the "real relation" among how the aggrieved understands itself as existing in a proprietary relationship to civil society, which in turn affords it the right to enact uncivility so that it can restore civil society to itself. That is, that political modality, when all the grievances of the aggrieved are dissolved, is ahistory. The natural and only appropriate order of being is reinstated and secured. It can then be safely projected into the eternal future that is the unchanging same.

The logic of grievance does not rise to the level of "high-sounding drama." But it unleashes within civil society a theater violent in its actions and violently unapologetic in its contradictions. What is at stake in this political theater is nothing less than the "state," at least, how the "state" is ordered and organized, and who has the power to decide on that ordering and organization. The theater of uncivility that erupts in civil society suggests not a break but rather a violent continuum between the two.

II.

For the aggrieved, alienation—as temporary, of course, removal from power—constitutes a subjectivity. In fact, the aggrieved can be said to emerge into history only in that moment when it proclaims itself alienated. That is, compelled out of ahistory into history. If, for Marx, alienation is the predictable effect of human beings finding themselves removed, cut off, from what they produce, then for the aggrieved alienation is anything but the natural effect of historico-economic forces.

It is, rather, the effect of the rude—crude—force of history. King George III's refusal to adjust the British crown's diktats to the realities—"needs"— of the thirteen colonies. The North's unrelenting demands that culminate in a war of aggression. The Negro's insistence that the terms of Reconstruction be implemented. The Negro and the North's refusal to accommodate the peculiarities of the South after World War I and II, not understanding that making the world safe for democracy was a solution applicable to a fratricidal Europe but must not be "imported" to US shores. Civil rights as an uncivil attack on the South's mode of being.

Aphorisms VI
Tolerance, Intolerance

> The distinction is between a personal ethic
> of tolerance, an ethic that issues from an
> individual commitment and has objects
> that are largely individualized, and a polit-
> ical discourse, regime, or governmentality
> of tolerance that involves a particular mode
> of depoliticizing and organizing the social.
> —Wendy Brown, *Regulating Aversion:*
> *Tolerance in the Age of Identity and Empire*

I.

If we follow Wendy Brown's argument about the depoliticization of tolerance, then we can assert that it is precisely the power of the state-derived authority to "depoliticize" that naturalizes griev-ance. Depoliticization provides the grounds for the justification of violence against the other. For the aggrieved, violence is made necessary by history. This allows the aggrieved to present its intolerance as a reconstituted right that justifies its actions.

II.

"Depoliticizing" derives, of course, from "politicizing."

And "politicizing" always represents the obstinacy of facts that stubbornly refuse to suborn themselves.

That is, facts are those articulations of truth that do not conform to the principles of the aggrieved.

Unhelpfully stubborn in their fidelity to truth, facts.

III.

Dastardly facts will not submit to the God who seeks vengeance in the name of righteous grievance. The God under which we supposedly stand, and to whom, behind the veil of the flag, we pledge allegiance.

Here we are better off hoping, with Nietzsche, that God is dead. And if this is indeed the God to whom allegiance is pledged, then it is better that God remain dead.

IV.

No doubt because it is losing its efficacy, "politicizing" is now on the verge of extinction, shuffling off the mortal coil of political usefulness.

Its replacement? "Weaponization." How ironic a term.

It is in the very attachment to this term that the gross comedy of grievance shows itself again. The proponents of making weapons universally available in the service of grievance claim to be on the side of depoliticizing as "de-weaponizing."

Mass shootings. The world's leader in mass shootings.

The rebuttal to calls not to disarm the populace—what a terrible idea!—but control the proliferation of weapons, to bring an end to mass shootings, assumes an infallible logic.

"Guns don't kill people, people do."

"Only a good guy with a gun can stop a bad guy with a gun."

More threateningly, "In Texas we don't call 911."

This is the supreme alternative among all alternative facts.

Infallible logic.

V.

An infallible logic that is intolerant of contradiction: "And it's not surprising then they get bitter, they cling to guns or religion or antipathy to people who aren't like them or anti-immigrant sentiment or anti-trade sentiment as a way to explain their frustrations."[21]

Guns, God, "antipathy" for the other, fear of capitalism's predations.

But hasn't the gun, along with an inviolable right to own and to arm, to own and to kill, long since reached God-like status? Is that not the truth of the Second Amendment? Does not the gun disempower God by allotting to human beings a sovereign right, to take a life? To take a life in the cause of protecting private property? Or for no good reason at all? Thou shalt be free to kill ... schoolchildren, their teachers, moviegoers, random strangers ... Without cause. Because you can. Because your right to possess arms is inviolable.

VI.

What is the order here? God, then guns? Or guns, then God? Or are they, as seems most likely, on equal footing?

Is the right to kill not the ultimate weaponization of God?

Is there not an alternative Holy Trinity? God, Guns, the Intolerable Other? When the aggrieved is armed in the name of God, the intolerable other, source of all grievance, can be put to the sword.

A new commandment I give unto you: kill the other. So that they might not multiply. In their fruitfulness they threaten you, My Chosen People.

God who makes out of American exceptionalism a new rule. A new covenant is made with his people.

For God so loved America that God created the semiautomatic to keep her safe from the other? To prevent the other from taking American jobs? To keep capitalism only advantageous to God's Chosen People?

Did this God decree that in things economic the United States should prevail? For God so loved America that God gave it special favored nation status in all economic agreements? So that America jobs would not be shipped abroad? So that only America would always be prosperous?

Is that what is meant by "God Bless America"? That the rest of the world can go about unblessed? Does God's exceptional love for America make God an inveterate provincialist, an unreconstructed nationalist? Small-minded, parochial, concerned with local matters? Attentive only to God's people?

Choose, God.

Once more, we would be wise to cast our lot with Nietzsche.

VII.

Unless, of course, God proclaims that those who take a life, who take lives, must expect no pardon.

God not as vengeful, but as equal in the distribution of justice.

Who could not abide such a God?

Only the perjurer, who has already committed all manner of violence against history.

We should long for a God in the mold of that God known to Abraham and Isaac. A God ruthless in the dispensation of justice. Maybe then the meek could indeed the inherit the earth, and the *truly* aggrieved too. And not a moment too soon. That moment when God distinguishes fish from fowl, fair from foul.

Can we save God from those who speak in the name of God?

VIII.

Is America the creation of a perjured god?

Is Puritanism a form of perjury? A false promise?

IX.

If America is the creation of a perjured god, is it therefore a nation beyond pardon?

Does repeated perjury automatically disqualify the aggrieved from pardon?

If not, then how many acts of perjury does it take? At what point can perjury expect no pardon?

Do the aggrieved consider themselves entitled to limitless acts of perjury without foregoing the possibility of pardon?

X.

What kind of god gives perjurers such license?

Until that moment of a transcendent, redistributive justice arrives, we are left to remark that grievance marks the limits of liberal tolerance.

The perverse tolerance for "weaponization" knows no limits.

XI.

Intolerance derives directly from grievance.

XII.

Grievance is that moment, that mode of being toward the other, when ahistory can only be preserved through intolerance.

XIII.

Intolerance is the willingness to confound liberal pieties.

Intolerance reveals the insubstantiality of liberal tolerance.

XIV.

Grievance licenses intolerance to act against those personages, ideologies, culture(s), religions, political claims, and those others who make the claims that threaten ahistory.

XV.

Intolerance marks that moment when grievance calls upon its political offspring, intolerance, to act in the name of an ahistorically unforgivable injury.

XVI.

Grievance marks that point at which the aggrieved self will no longer suffer—endure—the other.

For the aggrieved, intolerance marks the limit of sufferance.

Intolerance announces that moment when the aggrieved will no longer accommodate itself to the cause—life—of the other.

Intolerance announces the aggrieved self as finally unwilling to adjust to the sensitivities of the other.

XVII.

Intolerance is that moment when the aggrieved can tolerate injustice no longer.

XVIII.

Intolerance asserts the triumph of politics over the ethos of affect.

Intolerance is impatient with "feelings."

Intolerance follows Carl Schmitt: it distinguishes only between "friend and enemy." And it deals with each on ruthlessly appropriate terms.

XIX.

As such, intolerance is as unsparing in relation to the other's ethos as it is dismissive of those in its own ranks to whom it deliberately gives offense.

XX.

Grievance is, as Richard Rorty intuited, intolerant of any desire for an "improvement in manners."[22]

Grievance tears away the fig leaf that is self-righteousness.

The aggrieved know how to perform their pieties.

They proclaim themselves not aggrieved but beneficent. Acting in the cause of a greater good. Selfless, in addition to being self-righteous.

In its intolerance, grievance is, contra Rorty, proudly belligerent. It delights in being uncouth—intolerance is another manifestation of the uncivil.

XXI.

Intolerance is how the aggrieved reasserts its primal will to power.

XXII.

Grievance assigns intolerance the work of restoring the *nomos* after having run roughshod over the order imposed by history.

Intolerance is certain that it can, at the flick of a switch, restore the natural order. A self-affirming, intolerant order.

XXIII.

Grievance so enacted will disavow itself as

"uncivilized"—barbaric.

It will insist instead that its barbarism might be transgressive but constitutes a terminal, goal-oriented violence.

XXIV.

A just violence. Mobilized for the worthiest cause. The violence of the aggrieved is simply a means to achieve a just end.

XXV.

The violence of the aggrieved self is instrumental. The other's violence is inchoate. The other's violence is character-defining. The other's violence is fundamental to its being. The other's violence is pure ontology. Irremediable, transcendent, permanent.

The other's violence is a threat to all the aggrieved holds dear: democracy and everything else that the putative liberal self takes as its fundamental values.

XXVI.

In acting intolerantly, the aggrieved professes its commitment to *nomos*. The invocation of *nomos* announces to the other: so far, and not an iota farther. So much, and no more.

The commitment of the aggrieved to *nomos* stands as the reimposition of the natural limit. Once more, the restoration of ahistory.

XXVII.

Unlike tolerance, intolerance will not abide the incommensurable. Self will not reconcile itself to the other. Intolerance is grievance's final word on the refusal to tolerate the other.

Intolerance does not mark the creation of a political self. It announces the arrival in history of an identity that exists only because it is a victim of history.

XXVIII.

The figure of grievance is never new in history.

Rather, every iteration of the figure of grievance marks the emergence of a figure appropriate to its time. Every figure emerges as either the endorsement of ahistory or a challenge to history—as a challenge to the disorder of things.

XXIX.

Lest we forget, it is grievance alone that can give us the figure of the aggrieved.

The self acted against, injured, the self made victim by history. The aggrieved as a distinct political actor with a singular political profile.

XXX.

The discourse of grievance reveals itself to be an ever-changing, now expanding, then contracting, shape-shifting set of practices and articulations.

As the moment demands.

All of which revolve around a core of grievance(s) that is absolute and non-negotiable.

Grievance articulates the permissible and the prohibited. Grievance delineates the permissible and the prohibited as a set of absolute limits.

Grievance undertakes this work even as it acknowledges, reluctantly, the imprecise marking that is the limit.

XXXI.

Grievance politicizes intensely, in Brown's sense, the abrogated rights of the aggrieved.[23]

XXXII.

Grievance most certainly does not depoliticize itself as a practice or a discourse.

XXXIII.

Grievance insists upon itself as imbricated in the very core of the political. It insists upon itself as written into the nation's founding political document.

Grievance, as such, has long since declared itself.

XXXIV.

Grievance is not an appeal to power. It is rather

an abashed claim to power—a discursive, militaristic claim—that the aggrieved self considers an inalienable right. Grievance comes into its own at the precise moment when that inalienable right is denied. Grievance seeks to vanquish history. Once and for all. If that does not work, grievance will rouse itself again and again to do the work of overcoming history.

XXXV.

Grievance is assertive. It does not ask.

It demands. It takes.

XXXVI.

But not all demands, as is the case with grievances, are equal.

When the *sans culottes* storm the Bastille, that is a justifiable grievance.

When those who understand themselves to be aggrieved but are not storm the US Capitol, they do so without justification.

They do, however, reveal themselves in all their intolerant, intolerable violence.

XXXVII.

Intolerance proclaims the reanimation of the ahistory of that aggrieved political self that has been made vulnerable, made subject to history, by the other.

XXXVIII.

Intolerance renders the aggrieved political self as an avenging—vengeful—collectivity.

The intolerant claim for themselves a political self-understanding that locates their grievance in injury or victimization.

Most often, of course, the aggrieved know themselves to be simultaneously injured and victimized.

Aphorisms VII
Time and the Shaman

The righteous moralism that so many have registered as the characteristic political discourse of our time—as the tiresome tonality and uninspiring spirit of the Right, Center and Left—can be understood as the *symptom* of a certain kind of loss .... nothing is ever *merely* a symptom.
—Wendy Brown, *Politics out of History*
(original emphases)

I.
Every "symptom" of grievance must be apprehended as an unimpeachable claim.

II.
Every act of grievance is a response to an injured will.

III.
Every act of grievance constitutes, out of necessity, a recrimination against injury.

IV.
To ignore the "symptom," to fail to act in the face of injury, would be an offense to the ontology of the aggrieved. A blow to its very essence. A betrayal of

the commitment the aggrieved makes without ever having to utter a word, let alone speak a complete oath of fealty, to ahistory.

V.

That is the time the aggrieved is duty-bound to honor.

Without such a commitment, the aggrieved would have no choice but to abandon the present-past and enter history. Submit to the laws of teleology. Acknowledge that "time marches on." Relentlessly. Without regard for, trampling and riding rough-shod over, ahistory.

VI.

Ahistory is a stay against the prospective. A resistance to the disenfranchising now. A struggle against what-already-is but must-not-be-allowed-to-be. A struggle against the interruption of ahistory. A struggle against the irruption of history into ahistory.

VII.

Once more, rolling the boulder up against the hill of time.

As if that never-to-be moment when the boulder sits atop the hill will put an end to time.

The enemy of ahistory, time.

One is tempted to characterize the enemy as "Time."

A proper name fit for a formidable adversary. An immovable enemy, one deaf to entreaty, fully protected against any form of immanent violence. Unstoppable in its forward march.

VIII.

A march that, again and again, refuses to yield to the demands of ahistory.

A heartless enemy. Implacable. The spawn of modernity. The offspring of a ceaseless rationality that has no qualms about proclaiming, repeatedly, the triumph of Reason.

IX.

A Reason so devastatingly sure of itself. Unshakeable in its self-belief.

X.

An enemy that promises, if the contradiction might be permitted, no future for ahistory. In its most charitable moments, this enemy will permit of the envisioning of a bleak future, an ahistory attired in shabby, anachronistic garb.

An Aphoristic Interlude
The Shaman as
a Village Person

I.

Hairy-chested, beefcake naked, tattooed, wearing horned fur hat and stars-and-stripes warpaint, a spear in one hand and a US flag in the other, the shaman presents only minimally as a fearsome threat.[24]

II.

The shaman strikes one more as an image transported into 2021 from a gay pictorial magazine from the 1950s or 1960s.

III.

Or, should one have a preference for the gay culture of the 1970s, the shaman might be thought that gay character rejected by the Village People.[25] The Village People wanted people, real people. Not a human being who did not know that he wanted to be transformed into a wolf.

IV.

The Village People's Indigenous American (the "Indian"),[26] the G.I., the construction worker, the cowboy, and the biker (clad all in leather), for all their mustachioed machismo, not only retained a subtlety of character but also demonstrated a confident self-possession limned by a detectable note of self-irony.

V.

It always seemed as if they were sharing a joke, an in-joke, to be sure, but not so private that their fans could have no access to it. Maybe even share it, just a little. After all, during their heyday, only one of the Village People, the "Indian," was gay. (The "cowboy," Randy Jones, would later come out as gay too.) So the group was already constituted out of an in-joke.

VI.

The Village People seemed capable of laughing at the world. And at themselves.

VII.

The shaman's smile did nothing to disguise the air of brutal, militaristic violence that seemed to emanate from him, in his guise as Jake the (non-Edenic/Angelic) Snake. Not so much tempting others to follow his example as calling them to arms in a visage that was the unadorned face of aggrieved machismo. As if Chansley could not but assume his true guise: that of the avenging Angel-I.

VIII.

No wonder the shaman had need of so many names. He was called to duty by many masters. He endeavored, dutifully, to serve them all.

IX.

Knowing he could only serve all if he was equally threatening in every guise. But it was as the shaman that he was most threatening. That he threatened everyone outside his immediate orbit.

X.

Possessed of many guises, in the service of so many, still the shaman could never laugh at himself.

Gelos, the Greek god of laughter, remains unknown to the shaman.

The shaman, however, may be willing to take Gelos's Latin name, Risus.

After all, even if the name is unfamiliar and does not provoke laughter, there is no doubt that as a linguistic effect, Risus suits the shaman. Risus rhymes with crisis.

The shaman took great joy in overseeing crisis.

The history of America is such that grievance always appears on the verge of provoking a historic crisis.

XI.

A tragedy, this lack of capacity for self-deprecation? Or appropriate, given that he sought to lay the world to waste?

XII.

Ironic, this hypermasculinity that has not the self-awareness of itself as the parodying of hyper-masculinity. When the aggressive straight vigilante presents as a gay icon.

XIII.

The shaman, the gay Village Person no one ever heard of. With good reason.

The shaman, the gay figure for whom there is no place in the Pride parade.

The shaman is the gay figure without any sense of place.

Who goes to the US Capitol to celebrate Pride on a freezing January afternoon, clad in nothing but a loincloth and a Davy Crockett hat? The uncharitable would, of course, prefer that the shaman's loincloth be properly named: skimpy skirt.

XIV.

What a convergence: the grievance boys showing up in gay costume, determined to bring democracy down, only to present the world with a beefcake burlesque. What aggrieved boy wouldn't be proud of that?

XV.

A comical convergence in a Capitol farce.

The second coming of a tragic original.

XVI.

The edge just barely taken off the tragedy by the shamanistic evocation of the Village People. An image now made palatable, if only just, by the recognition that time and the Village People get the last laugh.

XVII.

We the people.

We the Village People.

We the Aggrieved People.

Ergo, We the Insurrectionist People.

XVIII.

The joke is on the shaman.

XIX.

But who was in the mood to laugh then? Or is now?

XX.

Maybe we can laugh a little now, but only if we attune our cultural antennae accordingly.

XXI.

Always keep your gaydar on when you're watching an insurrection.

Then you might discover a funny side to a violent spectacle.

XXII.

Time gets the last laugh.

As time moves on and we get lost in it, we forget to laugh. We forget the time of laughter.

We no longer remember how to live again in laughter.

XXIII.

Robert Plant: "Does anybody remember laughter?"[27]

XXIV.

The loss of time is also a cause of grief. To come to terms with loss, grief, without promoting grievance is a great difficulty, as it should be. A difficulty intensified by US national culture in our moment.

XXV.

We forget, woe unto us, how much fun it was to dance to "Y-M-C-A."

O disco, we do you wrong. Disco, you weren't a stairway to heaven, but you were a wonderful diversion in the decade that saw the oil crisis, the war grinding on in Vietnam, the beginning of the AIDS crisis, and anticolonial wars raging in Angola and Mozambique, among others.

The decade that gave us the Bee Gees, an unbelievably cool Stevie Wonder, the anthemic Gloria Gaynor, a gloriously young and unabashedly black Michael Jackson, the first strident notes of Bruce Springsteen, the soul of Earth, Wind and Fire, a Bob Dylan infatuated with Christian fundamentalism, the beat of Kool and the Gang...

The decade that really showed us how "get down on it."

XXVI.

In contrast to those delightful beats, the shaman leaves us with a palimpsestic gay archive of an insurrection. An archive produced out a series of images provoked into a concatenation across three decades. This leaves us with a store of images that are unerasable.

XXVII.

1950s–1960s gay pictorial beefcake, iconic 1970s gay band, a 2020s insurrectionist just begging, unbeknownst to him, to be included in this gay archive.

A gay science all our own. A gay science wonderfully, un-/ironically, our own.

XXVIII.

It is only through the gay science that the shaman can insert himself into history.

There is no place for the shaman as a gay icon in ahistory.

In ahistory the shaman would have to go by a more recognizable name. And no one of any note has yet entered ahistory with so quotidian, exaggerated, and unremarkable a moniker as Jacob Anthony Angeli Chansley.

XXIX.

For one, that's far too many names. This is doubly true if we go by the shaman's full insurrectionist name: QAnon Shaman. No one enters ahistory, and certainly not history, with a prefix that implies anonymity.

As for "Q," that just seems like an invitation to question every vestige of the identity of the aggrieved, even if the "Q" in "QAnon" is supposed to signal a deity-like entity that is omniscient. According to "Q's" acolytes, "Q" can certainly foretell the outcome of political events. Did "Q" know that things would end for the shaman with a forty-one-month jail sentence?[28] That the shaman, like the New Testament Peter in the Garden of Gethsemane, would repeatedly renounce his own convictions? Was this renunciation not simultaneously the disavowal of "Q"? The shaman balefully admitting the error of his Q-inspired ways?

XXX.

The ostensibly reformed shaman, now a vegan, who has given up beef. Do insurrectionists have to go to prison before they become vegans? If every insurrectionist followed the shaman's path, imagine how good that would be for the health of the planet. What economy of carceral housing. They'd all be in cellblock V: "V," not for *vendetta* but for vegan.

XXXI.

"Q," however, remains a mystery beyond us.

Is that why we are free to speculate that the selfsame "Q" also marks a certain Homeric futility? "Q" as the unfulfillable quest? Quest for what? The reinstatement of ahistory? It might also be that "Q" has been incorrectly gendered by the shaman and his like. Maybe "Q" stands for "Queen." A queen who likes beefcake. Is that possible? Does the shaman intuit this? Is that why he presents himself as the cross-dresser of ahistory?

XXXII.

Better to still the doubts. Better to keep at bay all the qualms about "Q's" gender. Better to remain in the service of an uproarious machismo. A machismo in a skimpy skirt. Or was the shaman just indulging, as the odd insurrectionist is surely entitled to do, in a little harmless role playing? Gender bending? With the watching world an audience. Every queen's dream, isn't it?

Better still to dispense with all formality and to contract. Shaman. Less is more. In ahistoric and historic terms.

XXXIII.

Could there be a more fitting ending for so tragicomic a figure, utterly blind to his own sexual self-resonance? A figure so lacking in self-awareness as not to know that he should have a beef with his status as beefcake?

A rhetorical moment fit for a queen. If, that is, the queen in question is Marie Antoinette. A Marie Antoinette pondering how to offer the insurrectionist masses "beef."

"Let them eat beefcake."

XXXIV.

The Capitol Rotunda as unwitting catwalk. A catwalk that, almost literally, the entire technologically connected world watched.

In horror.

This is where the "Macho Macho Man" struts his stuff.

You go, Beefcake.

XXXV.

Does anyone remember laughing then? In that moment, we were all forsaken by Gelos. "Laughter, does anybody remember laughter?"

XXXVI.

Was laughter impossible in the moment of shamanesque grotesquery because all who witnessed the spectacle were made party to it?

XXXVII.

Or rather, was that the sovereign moment of grievance? That moment in which the aggrieved came most fully into their individual and collective selves? That moment in which the aggrieved could collectively proclaim, *"Ich bin Groll"*[29]—"I am grievance"?

XXXVIII.

"Ich bin Groll" is an anachronism. *"Groll"* is a term that

probably belongs to seventeenth-century German. A term that has long since fallen out of usage.

XXXIX.

Therefore it is appropriate that we wrest it from centuries of neglect and refurbish it for the purpose of ahistory.

XL.

In this calculus it does not matter to which century the shaman properly belongs. It matters only that he has made the long-forgotten resonances of grievance—"*Ich bin Groll*"—audible to us again. By dragging us, against our will, against our better judgment, back to that century in which America was "founded."

XLI.

In "*Ich bin Groll*" we can, if we listen carefully, detect the earliest articulation of the aggrieved. The shaman was not so much reaching back—ahistory does not permit of that—as reenacting the original utterance of the aggrieved.

XLII.

The shaman made us hear that first call, in a language that might be most felicitous to that first call.

XLIII.

Jacob Chansley, the shaman who gives Angeli-c voice to ahistory.

Time and the Shaman, Continued

XI.

Is a consciousness entirely devoid of self-awareness the only reason that can explain why an insurrectionist presented himself as a shaman?

XII.

But then again, what choice did the insurrectionist have but to try to play a trick on time? To make time forget that it was supposed to march on when confronted by an insurrectionist who, it seemed, belonged to a different time altogether? A time more in keeping with ahistory? A time that the shaman could trust was organized for ahistory?

XIII.

Was the shaman but a valiant, if failed, attempt by ahistory to bring time to heel?

XIV.

Except, of course, we know that the shaman insur-rectionist was appropriating the time of an other, presenting as an other in order to fool time. The shaman belonged not to the time of the other but to modernity.

XV.

The aggrieved will assume any form so that it can give expression to its virulence.

The aggrieved are unashamed.

XVI.

But they are not yet unashamaned.

XVII.

Seeing so offensive an act of appropriation, so ridic-ulous an impersonation, time did not so much as pause. Not even for a moment.

XVIII.

Had anyone been paying attention amid the violence and the mayhem, there would have been audible a distinct sound: the raucous, mocking laughter of

Time disgusted by the imperatives of ahistory.

XIX.
Time ridicules the shaman as an impostor. A supremely modernist subject unable to confront that which is irretrievably lost.

XX.
Looking again on this atrocity, recognizing the foolishness that is ahistory, Time no longer laughs. It bellows with anger.

XXI.
And rightly so.
And not a moment too soon.

XXIII.
Would that Time could put a permanent end to ahistory.

Would that Time would be more effective in this project than Shakespeare's Hamlet. Called upon to act in a time of national crisis, Hamlet can only manage a vain hope: "The time is out of joint. O cursed spite,/That ever I was born to set it right."[30] And then proceed to fail, haplessly, if with spectacular dramatic results. A kingdom collapses because Hamlet cannot "set it right." In the moment of national crisis, Hamlet flailed about, desperate to find a language that could blend personal anxiety, the effect of a ghostly disclosure, and the demands of statecraft. In a state already pronounced "rotten."

XXIV.
(The aggrieved subject, it would appear, is possessed of a decisiveness and a determination entirely beyond Hamlet. To borrow Wendy Brown's terms, the aggrieved is a subject capable of "inciting" itself so that it can become a subject who can "overcome itself.")[31]

XXV.
That task, it appears, lies beyond even the sovereignty of time.

XXVI.
What a moment to fail us, Time. How untimely the limit of your sovereignty. What a violence to history is the outcome of your failure.

XXVII.
So subject to the sovereignty of time is grievance that in its logic, space is always made to follow the dictates of time.

XXVIII.
Within the logic of grievance, time defines space.

But that Time could deny ahistory.

XXIX.

That Time could act as though it too were aggrieved and unforgiving, and, most important, had no fear of consequences.

That Time would take offense at ahistory. That Time would apprehend ahistory as an intolerable assault on its historic sovereignty.

XXX.

That Time would strip away, rudely, the cloak of the shaman and in so doing reveal the shaman as nothing but the virulent "symptom" of a disease born within the body.

That Time would deny the aggrieved the right to present itself as made martyr by history.

That Time would uncloak the travesty against history that is ahistory.

XXXI.

That Time would no longer allow the aggrieved to perjure itself before the Court of Time.

That Time would impose its authority on ahistory.

That Time would take it upon itself to act violently against ahistory.

XXXII.

Why is Time so reluctant to act authoritatively?

Is it not said, as a smart turn of phrase in the vernacular, that "Time and Tide wait for no man?"

XXXIII.

What is Time waiting for? Better days? Why is Time so patient with this impostor, ahistory? Is Time not jealous of its sovereignty? Does the sovereign not reserve to itself, as Carl Schmitt teaches us, the power over life and death?

XXXIV.

Surely Time knows that its inaction gives life to the aggrieved and in so doing portends the death of the other?

XXXV.

Are we not justified to see ourselves, those of us who do not number among the aggrieved, as being let down by Time? Being made victim, advertently or not, by Time?

XXXVI.

Why now in this moment, of all times?

XXXVIII.

Why is it always the "best of times" for the aggrieved,

and the "worst of times" for the other?

Why is it always the other who feels the brunt of the unchanging same?

XXXIX.

Might the "slings and arrows" of time not, even if only occasionally, find a different target? Say, just now and then aim somewhere else? Is that too much to ask of Time?

Fragments III

> There should be a tension in the opposition between the state and democracy; a state should not simply be dissolved in democracy, it should retain the excess of unconditional power *over* the people, the firm rule of law, to prevent its own dissolution.
>
> —Slavoj Žižek, *In Defense of Lost Causes*

I.

Democracy is constitutively imperfect, Žižek argues. It is democracy's constitutive imperfection that makes it so dependent upon excess. It is for this reason that democracy inclines toward a singular urge: to make the state, the polis, the political, more democratic.

Democracy as a constitutive insufficiency. Democracy always needs more.

"The tree of liberty must be refreshed from time to time with the blood of martyrs and tyrants. It is its natural manure." Democracy abides all, even those conceived out of dung. American democracy has been from its inception indiscriminate. Dung, 1776, to dung, 2021.

Always alert to the ridiculous and the per-verse, Žižek capitalizes on the joke that democratic excess so readily lends itself to a fanciful neologism, "'deMOREcracy."

Would democracy crumble with less? Crumble if less blood is shed in its name? How much blood is enough?

Another joke presents itself, making light of that age-old democratic canard that insists that there can never be enough democracy. What would democracy be with less democracy? What Jefferson does not seem to ponder is whether the "blood of tyrants," by itself, will give rise to tyranny. Can the "blood of tyrants" overwhelm the by-now insufficient blood of "patriots"?

If there is to be a bloody struggle—between the American revolutionaries and the British colonists, between the Union and the Confederacy, between the Hatfields and the McCoys, between Bull Connor and Martin Luther King Jr.—will it matter whose blood wins? Is the winner the side that spills the most or the least blood? Surely military logic favors the latter. But Jefferson, unlike Tertullian, gives us no clue as to the metric by which he determines "liberty" can be preserved. And, from time to time, find itself given an infusion of blood that allows for growth.

What is democracy sans blood? Tyranny? A dictatorship? Rule by insurrection? Is it not likely that the tyrant will emerge out of the "manure" of insurrection? Can democracy forestall insurrection? Can it be restored after insurrection? Will the democracy that follows insurrection still be a democracy? Surely it cannot take itself to be the same democracy as before.

This last question especially assumes salience because it goes to the heart of the difficulty: What happens when democracy is unable to exert its institutional power "over" its insurrectionists?

On the face of it, democracy can accurately be designated an empty form. From which we can then conclude that its strength derives, paradoxically, from its weakness. The weakness of democracy is that it is not sufficient. Democracy, as we have determined, needs "more." This means that as an empty form, democracy is open to all political content.

Does this resonant weakness/strength in democracy explain why Americans of the liberal persuasion congratulate themselves that in the aftermath of the insurrection, the "institutions of democracy" are still "strong"?

The effect of such a political bromide is that the constitution of US democracy is never drawn into question.

Satisfied with the strength, putative or not, of its "democratic institutions," the United States fails to address the ways it dispenses justice. The ways it affords some rights—due process—but routinely denies others. Denies the other. The ways the state is willing to cede "power over (some) people" without thinking itself in the middle of an existential crisis.

How is it that when the aggrieved usurp power, or assert their right to usurpation, the state and the state of democracy are not considered in mortal danger? Even if the insurrection only presented itself as a spectacle, we know that the spectacle is never only a spectacle, much as the symptom is never only a symptom.

II.

Is the real link not between the state and democracy, but between a segment of the ruling constituency of the state, an inconstant segment, and the power that this segment understands itself as always having access to? In other words, is the real nexus not between democracy and the state, which is also a principal point of friction (out of which insurrection can arise), but rather a concatenation among democracy, the state, and race?

Idiomatic, surely, this concatenation. And yet not, because the insurrection of 2021 is, at least at the level of public discourse, always presented in its singularity, in its exceptionality. January 6 is presented as an aberration when it is, in fact, only the most recent exception. This makes it not so much an exception as part of a pattern, a distinctly American mode of being toward the state.

Democracy is rhetorical cover. The ascription of power to one constituency that is above all others and acts at the expense of all others. That is the rule of US democracy.

This means that it is already paradoxical, if not outright oxymoronic, to inveigh against the insurrection as an assault on democracy.

Surely such language cannot stand.

Surely the calculus is more straightforward: the white aggrieved is the only constituency in the history of the United States to presume itself entitled to attack the state when it fears, or even just imagines, that its power is being diminished.

Democracy, then, is not in the United States an empty form at all. It is full to the brim with grievance.

Which makes of America not a democracy but a state held, since its founding, in the thrall of grievance.

The most undemocratic of states because it recognizes as legitimate only one form of grievance.

All grievances are not, decidedly, in the United States, equal.

The other has no right to act on its grievance. The aggrieved have the right to enjoy turkey and pumpkin pie with their genocide. Should it chance to do so, the state will show itself as distinct from democracy.

The state will not hesitate to bring the full bore of its power to bear on anyone who does not conform to the profile of the historically aggrieved.

Power in the United States is only power when it needs to assert itself over the other.

The state of democracy in the United States is never drawn into question because it has always been, since the nation's founding, a settled matter. That is the logic—orthodoxy—of US democracy.

Any other critique of the state-democracy-aggrieved concatenation amounts to heresy.

It is not, to reconstruct Jacques-Alain Miller's argument, that "orthodoxy follows heresy."

The heresy is said to inhere in the suggestion that the United States is undemocratic. It is heretical to critique the double standard that is the implementation of US justice. It is certainly unthinkable to pronounce the United States constitutively aggrieved, to say nothing of the effects of the perpetuation, virulence, and adaptability of such grievance.

III.

USA: let us append the only proper name appropriate to it: the United State of Aggrieved.

Aphorisms VIII
Empathy

I.
Grief has the capacity to evoke in us empathy with the grief of others.

II.
Grievance is unto itself. It does not align itself, except for the sake of expedience, with the grievance of the other.

III.
The aggrieved understand their grievance to be grievance sui generis.

IV.
The grieving sense the possibility that, through

empathy, it might be able to forge a way forward, find its way to another time. Without ceding anything come upon in the time of grief to the time that comes after. All the while knowing that the time that comes after grief is saturated with the time of grief.

V.
The grieving know that time's forward march, inexorable though it might be, will always be marked with the being of *that* other time.

VI.
Knowing that time is so marked, the grieving can allow themselves to be always in the present time of being.

VII.
Grief knows that if it can be within the marked now it is already on the way to a mutual letting go that is also a loose embrace of, never a submission to, grief. Grief always has within it an openness to that time it does not know. That time to which it will not (yet) stake a claim.

VIII.
All the while, grief knows that it cannot lay claim to time. That time is for being, for being toward being, never for possessing.

VIX.

The aggrieved, by contrast, is intent on possessing, overwhelming, and subjugating time to its inflexible will.

X.

Out of a mutual letting go, something becomes possible. Out of a mutual letting go, whatever is mutual can develop. It can unfold, person by person, inoperative community by inoperative community.

XI.

"There are more things in heaven and earth, Horatio,/Than are dreamt of in your philosophy" (*Hamlet* 1.5.174-75). Grief is open to allowing things to come into their being. Into their fullness, even. Grief allows that things will happen as they will. In/ at their appointed time.

XII.

Grief is thinking a response to loss. Grief grapples with what it means to think loss. Grief asks us what it is to lose and raises for us, with unremitting intensity, what it means to have. Grief is the thinking of/ for dispossession.

Grief asks how it is, and why it is, we commit ourselves so to possession.

Grief has within it the capacity to laugh at us for

our foolishness that is our always insisting upon possession.

But grief, in its empathy, in making it possible for us to be as we have not been before (grieving), desists. It demands only that we think our grief. Grief instructs us into what it means to be open to what it is we do we not know. What we cannot know.

XIII.

What it is we cannot own.

Grief is an object lesson in dispossession.

XIV.

Grief opens vast new stretches of being before us.

It revels not in our ignorance but instead makes us confront what we do not know. In grieving, we can never know how we will think, what it is we will think about.

XV.

Grief makes us a promise. A one-of-a-kind promise, because it suggests, strongly, what it might make possible; it will not submit to transactional logic that can validate itself only through the signing of a promissory note.

Grief will only leave a trace of its signature.

And that is enough. Should always be enough.

Because of the trace we must always say, "What a trace."

XVI.
Grief intimates, very strongly, that we will be able to be, that we will be able to think, differently on the far side of loss.

XVII.
It intimates this without ever providing either an itinerary or a timetable; it provides no map; it has no schedule. It is punctual only to itself.

XVII.
Grief does not say *when*.

XVIII.
It leaves us with only the vaguest sense of certainty that we *will*.

XIX.
And that is enough, grief insists. It asks that we wait and see, learn what it means to endure.

XX.
But grief is not indifferent to our lack of moorings, so it offers solace by hinting at markings. It provides vague markings, occasional pointers, obtuse

intimations, each of which will allow us to make our way to that far side. In its own way, and strictly on its terms, grief attends to our needs.

XXI.

Grievance, by contrast, cannot wait.

It cannot wait for anything.

For grievance the present-past must be lived as an intense now, an intense now that revolves entirely around grievance.

XXII.

Grievance cannot wait because it must feel itself, it must feel itself intensely.

XXIII.

Grievance demands not only immediate redress but also an even more immediate address.

Grievance must be acknowledged. It must be spoken to, spoken of; it must, repeatedly and loudly, be allowed to speak itself. Not only in its own name— the grievance itself must be universally spoken.

Only in its ubiquity, in its dominating every sphere of public life, will grievance know itself as affirmed.

XXIV.

It is precisely in its bellicosity that grievance reveals

itself to have the temperament of an ill-mannered child.

XXV.

It is in his grotesque nakedness, his petulance, and his pathological need for public affirmation that the shaman with his love object most resembles such a child.

XXVI.

The child with the mock double phallus: spear in one hand, flag in the other.

Impotent in his rage. Does his loincloth hide a castration?

XXVII.

Is his castration, so poorly disguised, the historical reason for the shaman's grievance?

Has the shaman given himself to grievance because he does not, will not, learn how to grieve?

XXVIII.

Still, the shaman is a danger to all, despite his impotence. Or in truth, because of it.

XXIX.

Rage, rage.

Rage, the first and most belligerent enunciation of

grievance.

But is it an empty rage?

XXX.

It is only in his rage, the shaman seems to believe, that he can be seen. In his desperate need to be seen, he thrusts himself into our line of vision.

XXXI.

He cannot bear to be ignored.

XXXII.

Do we ignore him at our peril?

XXXIII.

Or do we imperil ourselves by acknowledging his rage?

XXXIV.

Or have we long since given up the possibility of a choice?

XXXV.

We have now arrived at that point where, regardless of how we apprehend the shaman, there is peril everywhere. Regardless.

XXXVI.

But is it really peril? Or is the shaman merely a

reminder that ours is the age of pathological need-iness? The shaman is of a piece with his Brioni-ed *Führer*, a septuagenarian so needy he created his own media platform to vent his grievance. The sha-man's capacity for need may or may not exceed that of Kim Kardashian, Kanye West, Marjorie Taylor Green, Lauren Boebert, Jimmy Butler, Alexandria Octavia-Cortez, Sinead O'Connor, everyone the world over who uploads a TikTok video ... the list is long. The inordinate neediness that breeds—and feeds—grievance makes bedfellows of them all.

There is no one on this list who would not be aggrieved if their public self were insufficiently recognized.

XXXVII.
Thereby lending an unmistakable emptiness to con-temporary grievance. A vacuity fueled by a particu-lar bitterness: the public nonrecognition of the var-iously aggrieved.

XXXVIII.
The bathos of grievance.

XXXIX.
In contrast, there is desperate grievance. Grievance born out of destitution, lived by those who know themselves to be, as the unhoused, as the poor, as

those without access to health care, living the reality of being citizens of a country that is at once the wealthiest and the poorest in the world. Like those on fentanyl in major US cities, who literally fold into themselves.[32]

XL.

In contrast, there are those retired, now decamped to sunny climes, who will take up any cause provided for them by social media. Rich in their land of plenty, they find grievance in that which is presented to them as "grievance."

We cannot, surely, designate the ennui of the rich a form of grievance.

XLI.

They are aggrieved because they fear their continued access to material excess will be halted.

In their fears their hopes are laid bare. In their hopes their fears are laid bare. More. And still more. Forever and ever. *A-more.*

They trace their grievance to whatever the latest figure of fear may be. Is said to be. Is, so to speak, scare-mongered into being. Grievance as an empty form so that it can be made to accommodate whatever is to hand, whatever is politically expedient. Whatever hope or fear can be exploited.

Theirs is a life in which fear and hope lie cheek by jowl. A life in which their anger, which is, to them, innately rational, is both motivated and assuaged by the fantasy of a life in which the other acknowledges subservience to the aggrieved. They are open to very little of the world, save their desperate dedication to the self and the exhortations of narcissistic demagogues who stoke their anger, feed their fear, and nurture their fantasies. Fears can be fed, hope can be offered. Sometimes all in the same moment, in the same speech act.

XLII.

Grievance: a volatile cocktail of hope, fear, anger, manufactured outrage, cause, faux cause, racism, the catastrophe that is demographics, all finding its articulation in fulminations of a false, unbelieving, holding-the-Bible-upside-down, Bible-selling messiah. The messianic, in the form of the Teutonic—the unbelieving German from Queens, NY. "He also poured out the coins of the money changers and overturned their tables. He told those who were selling the doves, 'Take these things out of here! Stop making my Father's house a marketplace!'" John 2:16–17.

XLIII.

How are the nominally unaggrieved not to laugh at the aggrieved? Not to mock the self-indulgence that bespeaks both their hopes and their fears? Not to be derisive about their anger? The ridiculousness of their fealty to the latest false white prophet? How are the unaggrieved not to wish for the doom of the aggrieved?

XLIV.
Yet we dare not dismiss their grievance, no matter its vacuity. There is nothing to do but attend to the dissolution of self that is the languor of the aggrieved. The ennui of aggrieved ennui.

We cannot overlook their grievance because too often we have seen what violence it can provoke.

XLV.
Maybe this is what Milan Kundera means when says, "When Man thinks, God laughs."

XLVI.
Given what Kundera's God is surveying, why ever would they not laugh?

There is a disproportionately incendiary relationship between the emptiness of the grievance and the amount of damage it can cause.

The other will not allow itself to laugh, at least not publicly, at the vacuity of the aggrieved, at the ennui of a Southern state of mind. Risus can cause crisis. It is for this reason that the other stifles the inclination to laugh at the frippery of the aggrieved, at the indulgence that is their ennui, at their Tennessee Williams-like hypochondria, because the other knows who pays the "butcher's bill." It isn't Stella.

Aphorisms IX
"God is not Dead."

I.

The shaman is the symptom of how grievance has made itself ubiquitous.

II.

Should we not grieve this?

And if so, would this not mean that we will have to learn, again, to grieve?

To learn to grieve as if we had never grieved before.

III.

What is the remit of grief?

IV.

Can our newly learned grief be made to accommodate

grief for the symptomatic shaman?

What is the worth of grief if it cannot hold within its ambit the symptomatic shaman?

V.

What happens to grief if it takes grievance unto itself?

Is grief transformed?

Contaminated? Does grief's encounter with grievance leave it bruised, battered, and unrecognizable to itself?[33]

VI.

Is the encounter between what we might take to be these two antagonists, grief and grievance, primal in their difference, a prototypically Nietzschean moment?

One of those moments when we are tempted to declare, "God is dead?"

VII.

Is it within the capacity of grief to dissolve grievance? To make grievance unrecognizable to itself?

VIII.

Out of its encounter with grief, does grievance undertake to learn grief? Does it recognize that it must now learn how to grieve?

Does grievance contemplate its own undoing?

Does grievance promise, to itself and all others, its own superannuation?

IX.

Is it possible that out of the encounter between grief and grievance God could come to life? That God could, out of sheer surprise at this unprecedented encounter between historic antagonists, rise to life?

X.

Is the only proper name for the dissolution of grievance into grief love?

XI.

Is it love, above all else, that grievance cannot bear?

XII.

Is love grievance's kryptonite?

XIII.

Is grief the solvent that grievance fears above all others? Does grief remind grievance of its own fragility? Of its own viscosity? Does looking on grief remind grievance how perilously close it always is to dissolution? Is grief what grievance finds not unrecognizable, but rather that to which it is closest, with which it is most intimate? Does grievance fear

that it contains within it, like a benevolent phar-
makon, always the germinating seed of grief?

XIV.
Does grievance live in fear not only of grief but also
of its precarious self?

XV.
Does grievance know that grief is what it would be
if it did not set itself so uncompromisingly against
grief?

XVI.
Is grief that which always lurks in the shadow of
grievance? Is grief not so much a stealthy (existential) threat to grievance as the intimate voice of an
invitation to dissolution?

XVII.
What mode of being sanctions its own dissolution?

XVIII.
But is that not what grief abides, even when at its
nadir? The possibility of the dissolution, the coming
apart, of the grieving self?

XIX.
If this is so, then surely one of the features that

distinguishes grief from grievance is that grief is not afraid of its own possible undoing.

Grief knows itself as that which can destroy the self. And still it persists, unwilling to submit to so existential a fear.

XX.
Grievance fears grief because it understands that, unlike itself, grief has no fear of itself. And if there is no fear of self, then surely there can be no self-loathing.

XXI.
Is grievance the public presentation of self-loathing in the guise of belligerent violence?

XXII.
Or do we ascribe to grievance a profundity it does not possess?

XXIII.
At what point should we caution ourselves against assigning to grievance qualities, depths of insight, it does not possess?

XXIV.
Let us agree to always be wary of grievance.

XXVI.

Let us commit to never shrink from thinking grievance. Even when grievance resists thinking itself.

Especially because grievance is so averse to thinking itself.

XXVII.

How else could we determine God's status? How else would we know whether God is dead or alive?

XXVIII.

After all, is that not the question that Nietzsche bequeathed to us?

And, as such, is it not the question we must always strive to answer? At the very least, the question we must not fail to address?

XXIX.

But is there not another question that lurks in the one about the status of God?

Another question that turns, as it must, on what distinguishes grief from grievance?

XXX.

Is grief not only the repository of love but also, more importantly, salient due to its capacity to enfold within itself the possibility of being?

At the very least, can we not assert that grief aspires to being? To know being? To think being? To think how to be toward, for, the time of being? To make being always that which defines it? That which it takes as its horizon?

XXXI.
Is being what is foreclosed to grievance? Is this foreclosing what grievance chafes most strenuously against? Does grievance know that it does not know how to be toward being?

XXXII.
Does grievance know that being is foreclosed because being is always open to time, to the unfolding of time, and grievance cannot permit of time other than as ahistory? That is, grievance is the denial of time because time cannot be, except as the openness to being?

XXXIII.
There is nothing within grievance that inclines it toward being, toward the being of and for being.

XXXIV.
And if grievance will not incline toward being, can we then not presume that it substantiates Nietzsche's proclamation, "God is dead," without ever attending

to the question of being? Grievance cannot ask what "is" is. That is a question it will not abide. Is that because it is the question upon which grievance will founder? To disregard this question, to refuse to address it, will surely have grievous consequences.

XXXV.
Such as being able to declare, without a trace of Nietzschean hesitation, without Zarathustra's intense self-reflection, patinaed by at least a smidgeon of uncertainty, "God is dead."

XXXVI.
Without apprehending that Nietzsche's declaration, for all its apparent boldness, means not to resolve anything but instead to open us to the most urgent question: How are we to be in the world?

XXXVII.
Grievance offers one possible mode.

Grief presents us with an entirely different set of possibilities.

XXXVIII.
Faced with so conflicting a choice, we know, we have always known, that there can be no avoiding the decision.

XXXIX.

How are we to be?

Notes

1. As quoted in Tony Horwitz, *Confederates in the Attic: Dispatches from the Unfinished Civil War* (New York: Vintage, 1998), 153.
2. Bob Dylan – The Night They Drove Old Dixie Down Lyrics | Genius Lyrics, June 29, 2023. In the summer of 2023 a minor brouhaha occurred when it was reported that Dylan had once sung "Dixie" during a film shoot. See Bob Dylan Once Covered the Racist Song 'Dixie' (msn.com), July 2, 2023.
3. Quotable Church History — "The blood of the martyrs..." | YINKAHDINAY (wordpress.com), July 7, 2023.
4. Garry Wills, *Inventing America: Jefferson's Declaration of Independence* (New York: Doubleday, 1978), xxiv.
5. In his introduction to Jean-Jacques Rousseau's *The Social Contract and The Discourses*, Alan Ryan reflects on Rousseau's concerns about inegalitarian societies: "it is even more essential that society should be strongly egalitarian, since the more diverse people's interests become, the harder it will be to decide whether any given rule is general in the required sense" (Ryan, "Introduction," in Jean-Jacques Rousseau, *The Social Contract and The Discourses*, translated by G. D. H. Cole [New York: Knopf, 1993], xlii). In our moment, of course, there has been both a putative contraction and an intensification of Rousseau's concerns. The diversification of the nation, especially in the West, has not only expanded the range of "people's interests" but also contracted into the difficulty of "diversity." Different people living with each other within a single nation's borders also expands—and indeed, intensifies as never before in history—the range of possibility for grievances. However, inegalitarianism persists in terms of the monopoly on grievance.
6. As quoted in Wills, *Inventing America*, xxxii.
7. Jacques Derrida, *Monolingualism of The Other Or The Prosthesis of Origin*, trans. Patrick Mensah (Stanford, CA: Stanford University Press, 1998), 16.
8. Jay Fliegelman, *Declaring Independence: Jefferson, Natural Language, and the Culture of Performance* (Stanford, CA: Stanford University Press, 1993), 206.
9. Ulysses S. Grant, *Memoirs and Selected Letters*, ed. Mary Drake McFeely and William S. McFeely (New York: The Library of America, 1990), 735. "I felt like anything rather than ..." Robert E. Lee Quote (quotescosmos.com), July 4, 2023.
10. Evan Thomas, *Road to Surrender: Three Men and the Countdown*

to the End of World War II (New York: Random House, 2023), 10.

11. The unique force that the pronoun has assumed in our moment is of course its own story. It is a political question more than deserving of extended critique, in need of its own dedicated meditation.

12. Here it is worth remembering the Radical Republicans, who belonged to the same party as Lincoln, strenuously opposed the president in his attempts to placate the South, at the expense of the newly emancipated slaves. Notable among them are: Senator Benjamin Wade (OH), Senator Charles Sumner (MA), and Congressman Thaddeus Stephens (PA).

13. Southern Historical Society Papers, Volume 10, The men who wore the gray. (tufts.edu), June 30, 2023. In *Confederates in the Attic* Horwitz remembers, as a union organizer in Mississippi, encountering a monument in the state that read "The Men Who Wore the Gray Were Right and Right Can Never Die" (190).

14. Fliegelman, *Declaring Independence*, 36.

15. Melanie Miller argues for the importance of Gouverneur Morris in the drawing up of the Declaration. Morris, Miller contends, has been wrongly overlooked in his contribution. See Miller, *An Incautious Man: The Life of Gouverneur Morris*, Wilmington, DE: ISI Books, 2008.

16. https://www.goodreads.com/quotes/15042-the-truth-was-obscure-too-profound-and-too-pure-to, July 3, 2023.

17. Thomas, *Road to Surrender*, 55.

18. This Day in History: "If this be treason, make the most of it!" (taraross.com), July 1, 2023.

19. Wills, *Inventing America*, 63.

20. Martin Heidegger, *What is Called Thinking?*, trans. Fred Wieck and J. Glenn Gray (New York: Harper & Row, 1968), 4.

21. Obama says gun owners are bitter clingers; Supporter now says we're racist anti-Semites | Buckeye Firearms Association, July 9, 2023.

22. As quoted in Wendy Brown, *Regulating Aversion: Tolerance in the Age of Identity and Empire* (Princeton, NJ: Princeton University Press, 2006), 16.

23. Brown writes: "if politicizing identity 'occurs' at the point where the liberal promise of universal personhood (and all of its attendant goods) is found hollow, might the injury foundational to such identity contain not simply jealousy and disappointment but also persistent, yet thwarted, desire?" (*Politics Out of History*, 53). In thinking how the aggrieved understand rights as being inviolable to themselves it thus becomes possible to explicate

the link among "thwarted desire," inviolable, ahistorical rights and violence. If the desire of those who proclaim themselves holders of an ahistorical right is thwarted, then any response to the attack on the rights of the aggrieved is a priori not only justified but indeed preordained. It is part of the covenant the aggrieved made with ahistory.

24. Part of the reason that the shaman presents as less threatening is because he might, in truth, be more of a "hairy twink" than a beefcake. A "twink" is a thin young guy with some hair on his chest. We will, however, insist on the shaman as a "beefcake," because it allows us to make fun of him, casting him mirthfully and so directly against type. What do you "twink" of that, shaman?

25. The Village People, founded by a French producer, Jacques Morali, took its name from the famed avant garde/alternative/hipster community Greenwich Village in New York City. Greenwich Village is, of course, the downtown New York City neighborhood where the Stonewall riot took place in June 1969.

26. The Village People's 'Indian' Remembers Stonewall - Bloomberg, July 13, 2023.

27. Robert Plant's Change of Heart Over His Classic Led Zeppelin Stage Quip 'Does Anybody Remember Laughter?' (cheatsheet.com), July 6, 2023.

28. 'QAnon Shaman' Jacob Chansley sentenced to 41 months in prison for role in US Capitol riot CNN Politics, July 12, 2023.

29. I owe the history of this term to Dirk Uffelmann. However, he is not entirely sure when the term was most in use or fell out of favor. The critique that the term enables, then, represents a moment of linguistic opportunism on my part. Dirk is innocent in all regards.

30. William Shakespeare, *Hamlet* (London: Methuen, 1982), 1.5.196-97.

31. Wendy Brown, *Politics Out of History* (Princeton, NJ: Princeton University Press, 2001), 29. Brown's concept, "negative political investments," might be repurposed here to acknowledge the willingness of the aggrieved to act, without regard for consequence—itself of course a historic privilege of the aggrieved. The preparedness of the aggrieved to act is, Brown would insist, entirely rooted in its unquestioned right to citizenship; to enjoy, as it were, the rights of "free men and women" that is felicitously afforded them and, by contrast, routinely denied those whose claim to citizenship is regularly dismissed or compromised by history.

32. To deprovincialize, if only momentarily. A perfunctory list: Ukraine, Putin, black Africans in Tunisia, minority youth in France. Ours is a world where the dominant image is grievance. But not all grievance is equal.

33. Here I am invoking the opening lines of Bruce Springsteen's "Streets of Philadelphia." "I was bruised and battered, I couldn't tell what I felt/I was unrecognizable to myself" (https://www.azlyrics.com/lyrics/brucespringsteen/street sofphiladelphia.html#:~:text=%20Bruce%20Springsteen%20 Lyrics.%20%22Streets%20Of%20Philadelphia%22.%20I,me%20 wasting%20away.%20On%20the%20Streets%20of%20Phila delphia, July 7, 2023).

Also available from Prickly Paradigm Press: